A Reader's Guide

Harvey S. Wiener
Marymount Manhattan College

Charles Bazerman
University of California, Santa Barbara

HOUGHTON MIFFLIN COMPANY   Boston   New York

Editor-in-Chief: Pat Coryell
Senior Sponsoring Editor: Mary Jo Southern
Senior Associate Editor: Ellen Darion
Senior Project Editor: Janet Young
Editorial Assistant: Nasya Laymon
Senior Manufacturing Coordinator: Sally Culler
Senior Marketing Manager: Nancy Lyman

Cover design by Diana Coe.

Credits:
Pages 18–21: From *Economics* by William Boyes and Michael Melvin.
Copyright © 1991 by Houghton Mifflin Company. Reprinted by
permission.
(Credits continue on page 184.)

Library of Congress Catalog Card Number: 98-72092

ISBN: 0-395-87076-3

123456789-DC-02 01 00 99 98

Contents

Preface

Perhaps the most persistent demand on college students is the demand made by reading for course work. As you've no doubt already discovered, hundreds of pages of reading—textbooks, novels, poetry, and journal selections, just to name a few—await you regularly. Keeping up with course content means keeping up with your reading.

We have designed *A Reader's Guide* to help you get what you need for course success from the reading assignments your instructors make throughout the term. Each course will require the application of particular skills and abilities, and these no doubt will vary from one discipline to another. Just compare a couple of pages from a psychology text to a reading for a history course, and the differences will strike you immediately. Yet common strategies will underlie your approach to any readings you do.

You must always be on the lookout for the main idea, or theme, of the selection.

You must constantly refresh your working vocabulary by adding new words you've learned from what you read.

And, as a thoughtful, analytic reader, you need to draw appropriate inferences and to make correct generalizations.

Our book highlights the general techniques and strategies you'll need to work your way through complex college readings so that you don't miss important elements as you navigate extensive assignments on a regular basis. We explain each skill clearly and demonstrate it with interesting examples drawn from a wide variety of course texts. We've divided the book into four units for ease of reference: Comprehension, Interpretation and Evaluation, Basic Study Skills, and Vocabulary. The detailed table of contents and the index can help you locate the skills and strategies you need to work on. Also, we give each skill a number and, sometimes, a letter, according to the chapter that explains the skill. For example, in section b of Chapter 4, we explain how to find main ideas in paragraphs. The number and letter **4b,** then, refer to the section you need to examine for help in finding paragraph main ideas. When you are reading one section, the book may cross-refer you to another section by using the number of that other section.

Used in conjunction with your other courses, *A Reader's Guide* will help you read successfully at college.

Acknowledgments

We have many people to thank for their ideas on the preparation of this text. Colleagues scattered around the country have made thoughtful suggestions and have guided us in writing this book. We are grateful to

Brenda U. Beal, Genessee Community College
Mary Anne Borrelli, Connecticut College
Judith Schein Cohen, University of Illinois
Jayne Decker, University of Maine, Farmington
Bruce H. Foster, Rowan University
Sandra Schweighart Goss, University of Illinois,
    Urbana-Champaign
Linda Markels, DeVry Institute of Technology
Teresa Massey, Spokane Falls Community College

Christopher L. Miller, University of Texas, Pan
American
Maggi Miller, Austin Community College—
Rio Grande
Michael Moore, Georgia Southern University
Patricia Rottmund, Harrisburg Area Community
College
Randy Waterman, Richland College

—*H. S. W.*
—*C. B.*

Unit One

Comprehension

1

The Reading Process: An Overview

Careful reading draws on a complex set of strategies. Good readers rely on many skills in using the *reading process*—the overlapping steps and techniques that aid your understanding of the printed page. These strategies help you get the most out of what you read.

Throughout this book, you will examine the reading process as you explore major reading skills and learn how to read effectively for your college courses. In this overview chapter, you will learn steps to take *before* you read, *while* you read, and *after* you read. Following these steps will help you become an active reader. (Later in the book, you will investigate these skills more widely and deeply.) We have designed this book to help you practice the reading process; read better for your college courses; and in general, be an active, involved reader.

1a What to Do Before You Read

- **Find out what you know about the topic.** (See **2a**.) Prior knowledge—that is, what you know of a subject in advance—affects how well you understand and appreciate your reading.

Before you begin to read any selection, try to determine what the selection is about.

- **Look at the title and subtitle.**
  The title is often a gold mine of information about the reading. What does the title mean? Look at any subtitles for clues to meaning.

- **Look at graphs, photos, drawings, and charts.**
  What do these visuals tell you in advance about the selection? (See **3**.)

- **Look at the writer's name and at any information given about him.**
  What do you know about the writer? How can this information help you with the selection?

- **Read the first couple of sentences or paragraphs.**
  What is the writer trying to say? How do your own experiences and knowledge relate to the words you are reading?

- **Have a purpose for reading.**
  Establish a valid reason for reading. Do you want to learn new concepts and vocabulary? something about a topic you haven't explored fully before? someone's opinions on an issue? Are you checking an idea you have for a research paper?

  You can have more than one purpose, and you can change your purpose as you read. But the point here is that when you know your purpose in reading, you can focus more clearly on the task.

- **Look carefully at information and questions that may appear with the reading.**
  You may find key words defined in the margins or before or after the reading. You may see instructions telling you about the questions to think about at the start or the end of the piece. Looking at information and questions before you read can help you see what the topic is. These features allow you to reflect on other reading that

you may have done on the subject. You might also think of a personal experience that could help you understand the topic.

In **2a** you will find many more ideas for *prereading* (previewing) a selection.

1b   What to Do While You Read

- **Jot down what you are thinking.** (See **12.**)
  What do the ideas make you think or feel? Does the material support or challenge your own ideas on the subject? What questions come to mind as you read? Underline, highlight, or copy any words and sentences that impress you.

  The surest sign of an active reader is a person with a pencil, pen, or highlighter in hand. (See **12.**) If you own the book you're reading, write all over it—in the margins, on the inside front and back covers, between the lines. Blank paper is also a great aid, just in case you need space to develop an idea and let your thoughts wander.

- **Identify the writer's main point.** (See **4.**)
  All active readers regularly ask themselves one basic question as they read a selection: What is the main idea here? Sometimes the main point is very clear; in other cases, you have to figure out on your own what major point the writer is trying to make.

- **Be alert to vocabulary.** (See **14** and **15.**)
  Like paints for a painter, words are a writer's main tools, and the writer chooses them with great care and attention. All words have a concise dictionary meaning—the *denotation* of a word—and a more complex suggested or implied meaning—the *connotation* of a word. (See **15c** and **15d.**)

For example, a writer could use one of the following words to refer to a person who teaches: *teacher, professor, expert, specialist, tutor, mentor, lecturer, scholar, instructor, master teacher, student teacher.* Yet each word or phrase differs to some degree from the others and suggests meanings that go beyond a dictionary definition.

Active readers always think about vocabulary and weigh the reasons why a writer chooses one word over another. You also should pay attention to how well the words make you see and understand the points. *Images* (word pictures) add life and clarity to a writer's presentation. Are the images fresh and vivid? Is the vocabulary right for the topic? Or is it too simple? too stuffy? too complicated? Is the writer long-winded when more concise writing would do? Are the words so loaded with emotion that you can't weigh the issues calmly?

■ **Decide what you think the writer's reasons are for writing.** (See **10**.)
What is the writer trying to achieve? Does he want to make you laugh? make you think? entertain you? tell you a story? make you act? change your opinion? Once you know what the writer's purpose is, you can focus on how he tries to reach that goal.

■ **Determine the audience—that is, who the writer thinks will be the main readers of the piece.** (See **10**.)
In textbooks, of course, the writer's audience is the student. Yet you will read a wide variety of books in college, and the audience the writer sees in her mind will affect the writing strongly. Considering the intended audience, the writer makes key decisions about words and sentences, the main idea, the purpose of the selection, and so on.

- **Pay attention to the writer's tone.** (See **10**.)
  Tone is the writer's attitude toward the subject. When you know how the writer feels about the subject, you can better understand key elements, such as word choice, sentence structure, and style. And you can keep a cool head, even though the writer might feel strongly about an issue.
- **Consider the form of the selection.** (See **6**.)
  The *form* of a piece of writing is its shape. How has the writer put the article, essay, story, chapter, or poem together? How has the writer put the ideas together in a paragraph? Does he compare, describe, narrate, show causes? Do the sentences flow logically and naturally? Look at the introduction and conclusion. Do they hold your attention? Does the introduction pull you into the writing? Does the conclusion summarize or emphasize the writer's main points? Do all the ideas build from the main idea?

1c   What to Do After You Read

- **Think at length about the reading.**
  Check your earlier impressions. Were you right in your view of the main idea? Did the reading fulfill your purpose? Did you learn what you expected to learn? What thoughts and feelings did the selection leave you with? Did the writer accomplish her goal, as far as you are concerned? If the writer tried to convince you of something, are you convinced? If he tried to describe or narrate an event, can you see it clearly in your mind? If the writer tried to explain why something happened, do you understand why it did? If she tried to show how to do or make something, could you

carry out the steps? Don't leave the reading without trying to figure out what you just learned!

■ **Write down your impressions.** (See **12**.)

Produce a summary. Write a sentence or two explaining the main idea of the piece in your own words. Using a reading journal (see **12e**) will help you record thoughts informally and keep track of them.

■ **Take time to answer any questions accompanying the readings.**

The book you're reading may offer study questions, or your instructor may provide questions for you to answer. If you have produced questions of your own, try to answer them now that you have finished reading.

■ **Talk to someone about the selection.**

Raise with others the topic you read about. See what your roommate, friends, or instructor thinks of the main idea of the piece. Set up a study group to share ideas on your reading. Discussing what you read can expand your views and improve your understanding.

The Reading Process for Active Readers

Before You Read

● Tap into your prior knowledge of the topic. Examine the titles, subtitles, photographs, drawings, charts, maps, and other features for clues to the topic. Look at any vocabulary presented in boldface, in the side margins, or before the selection. Read the first paragraph and think about it before reading further.

● Determine your purpose for reading before you begin.

- Look carefully at instructions, questions, and any other information about the reading.

While You Read

- Write down your thoughts, impressions, and questions as you read.
- Identify the writer's main point, the main idea of the selection.
- Be alert to vocabulary.
- Determine the writer's purpose, the reason she had for writing the piece.
- Think about the audience, the group the writer had in mind when writing.
- Think about the tone of the piece: What is the writer's attitude toward the subject?
- Consider the form of the selection by examining the introduction, the conclusion, and the structure of paragraphs.

After You Read

- Think at length about what you have read.
- Write down your thoughts and impressions.
- Answer any questions.
- Talk to someone about the reading.

 APPLICATIONS: Your Courses

Be an active reader. As you read your assignments for your courses, keep the reading process in mind and apply the steps given.

2

Reading Aids

As part of the reading process, most experienced readers use prereading and other strategies to improve understanding.

- **Prereading** is a convenient term for all the steps you can take to prepare yourself before you actually read, such as making lists of questions and concept maps of what you already know about the subject.
- **Skimming** a selection means that you search quickly through the sentences to find the main facts—and answers to any questions you may have—before you begin reading closely.
- **Previewing** a selection involves looking at titles, headings, art, and other key elements to get a general idea of what you're going to be reading—again, before you actually begin reading. Previewing is useful for short selections, such as book chapters, stories, articles, or essays, as well as for whole books and magazines.

You can use these strategies to get a good sense of the materials you plan to read for your various courses.

2a Preread

Aware readers always draw on their *prior knowledge,* what they know about a topic before reading the selection. Prereading—thinking in advance about a topic before you read—helps you prepare for the words on the page. If you consider the topic beforehand, you'll find the writer's ideas a little more familiar than if you jump into the reading without prior thought. Your own knowledge helps you understand what the writer is saying.

For example, suppose you are ready to read a chapter about the nature of motivation in your psychology textbook. Think about motivation. What do you know and feel about motivation? How do you get motivated? What have teachers done to motivate you? How do you motivate yourself? How can you motivate a stubborn friend? As you think about these issues before you read, you remind yourself of what you already know. You also stimulate your own interest and curiosity. You get your mind ready to take in new information.

As a warm-up for reading, just let your ideas about the writer's topic flow before you start reading. Write down your thoughts. Make a list. Draw a word map. Use freewriting. Raise questions.

2a(1) *Make a List*

Make a list of everything that comes to mind when you think of the topic of the reading. For example, a student in a history class wrote the following list before reading an article on politics during World War II.

Politics During World War II

Who were the political leaders?
Was Franklin Roosevelt president of the U.S.A.?
Hitler
Nazis—took control of German government

Germany conquered most of Europe—France,
   Poland
D-Day—America and the Allies start to regain
   Europe
What to do with Nazis after the war? Political
   problem
Pearl Harbor, Japanese bombing
Who led Japan? Didn't Japan have an emperor?
Kamikaze fighters, battles in the Pacific
Atom bomb dropped on Japan—Hiroshima
Nuclear weapons became a big political issue in
   the U.S.A.
Political alliance among Italy, Germany, and Japan
Allies—U.S.A., England, France, other countries
Didn't the Soviet Union switch back and forth?
Political results of the war—splitting of Europe
   between East and West

   Notice how the student just follows her thoughts,
with one idea or name leading to another, and brings
into her conscious mind much information she
knows on the subject.

2a(2) *Draw a Word or Concept Map*

Drawing a word map or concept map is like making a list, but it helps you organize your thoughts
visually.

Put ideas down on a piece of paper, with related
   words and concepts close to each other.
Draw lines between connected ideas.
Use boxes, circles, arrows, or any other visual symbol to show how ideas can be connected.

   For example, a student about to read an article on
the business of sports made the word map shown on
page 12.

2a(3) *Do Freewriting*

Freewriting helps stimulate thinking on a subject. Simply start writing and write whatever comes into your mind. Do not stop. Don't worry about complete sentences. Don't correct words or revise what you say. Even if you can't think of what to write, just keep your pen moving. You can even write things like "I don't know what this topic is all about" or "I have forgotten everything I know about this." Soon one statement will lead to the next, and you will be surprised by how much you find you know.

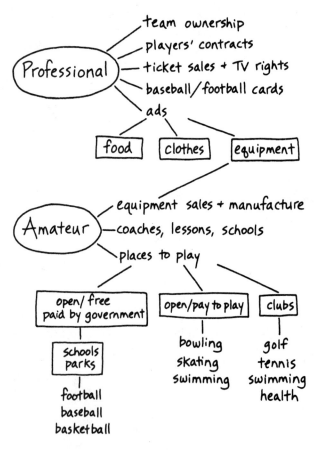

Freewriting also allows you to explore your feelings and interests, so that you can find points of connection between the subject of the reading and those things you would like or need to know about. Consider one student's freewriting prior to reading a chapter assigned for a biology course:

> Ugh! A chapter on flatworms. How gross. I'm just taking this course to fulfill my science requirement, and they keep giving us all this gross stuff to read about. If I try to skip over this chapter, I'll be lost for the rest of the term, because the teacher is making connections between simple organisms and more developed ones. It's weird to think that humans have some of the same systems as flatworms. They eat and breathe and excrete. Sometimes they do it a little differently than humans, but both flatworms and we have to solve some of the same basic problems of staying alive. It's sort of interesting to see the various ways these simple animals have developed biologically to carry out basic life functions. Maybe if I don't pay so much attention to them being disgusting worms, but instead think of them as certain ways of being alive, maybe I can understand all those details.

2a(4) *Raise Questions*

Another way to focus in advance on the topic of a reading selection is to write a list of questions that you would like to have answered about the subject. Before reading an article on violence in American history for a sociology course, one student wrote out the following questions:

Is America really more violent than other countries?

Do television and movies create the violence or only reflect it?

Who are the violent people and what makes them violent? Do violent people tend to come from any particular social groups? Is the violence caused by social pressures? Is violence an individual behavior or a group's way of life?

Do the ways my friends and I behave fit in with this pattern?

Are there any positive social functions of violence, or is it all negative? Do violent rock videos provide some positive entertainment and emotional release? How about violence used by the police or army? Don't these organizations help maintain social order?

Notice how, as the list of questions goes on, the student's special concerns appear. She moves from just blaming American society and particular groups to wondering how she might be involved in violence. From there she begins to wonder whether there might be some good to violence.

 APPLICATIONS: Your Courses

Choose a reading assignment in one of your courses. Explore your interests in the topic by making a list, drawing a word map, freewriting, or asking questions. Consider which technique worked best for you. Which do you think the choice of a prewriting method depends on: the kind of material you are reading or the academic course?

2b   Skim Readings

Rapid reading for facts is called *skimming*. Whenever you have to find *specific* facts in a paragraph, skim for sentences that offer the needed information. When you skim a paragraph or a page, you are searching quickly for the answer to some question you have.

Skimming: Finding Facts Quickly

- Make sure that you know what information you are looking for. Ask yourself a question. Look for a key word.
- Move your eyes quickly from line to line and from sentence to sentence.
- When you think you've found what you are looking for, *stop*.
- Slowly read the part of the line or sentence that tells you what you want to know.
- Think about the question you were trying to answer.
- Does the information you found answer the question? If not, quickly read the passage again to look for the information you need.
- Jot down the answer to the question you've asked.

2c   Understand Textbook Aids

Textbook writers and publishers now build into their books a number of special aids. Using these aids will help you get the most out of your reading.

■ **Vocabulary helpers.** (See **15g**.) At the beginning or the end of a chapter, you may find a list of key words or terms. Sometimes the author supplies definitions; at other times you have to check meanings on your own. You may also find a dictionary of key terms in a glossary at the end of the textbook. Some writers will highlight key words through boldface print or color type or will identify and define major words through notes in the margins.

- **Chapter or section goals**. A list of goals often appears before a chapter or section in your textbook. The goals identify the main points that the writer will address and help you focus your reading.
- **Drawings, photographs, charts, special displays**. To supplement, illustrate, or review principles in the text, a variety of visual displays can enhance your reading. These illustrations further explain information already presented in the text or present new information in easy-to-read formats.
- **Headings and subheadings.** In special print or second-color ink, headings and subheadings divide a textbook page into small units and also identify in a word or phrase the basic area of coverage.
- **Summaries.** End-of-unit summaries highlight key information and restate briefly the major issues the writer has addressed in the unit.
- **Bibliographies, "works cited" lists, or suggested further readings.** The author will often provide a list of resources or recommended readings that can add to the information presented in the chapter or section.
- **Study questions.** Study questions in short-answer or essay format help you test your knowledge and expand your thinking on the topics.
- **Textbook ancillaries.** Especially in courses like psychology, accounting, mathematics, and science, publishers will often provide special study aids as ancillaries—supplements (additions)—to the textbook itself. You may find a separately bound *study guide* to help you master the course material, *computer software* to help you review and test yourself on various chapters, and *laboratory manuals* to guide you through experiments and field work.

APPLICATIONS: Your Courses

Examine a textbook for a course you are currently taking and make a list of the special aids in the book.

2d Preview a Selection

Other helpful steps to take in order to read for information come *before* you actually begin reading. You can *preview*—that is, look ahead to the content of a passage—in a number of ways.

How to Preview a Reading Selection

- **Look at the title.**
  Always consider the title before you read. Titles often suggest the topic or the main idea of the selection and help you set a purpose for reading.
- **Look for headings.**
  Essays, newspaper articles, and other longer readings sometimes offer help in finding information by inserting *headings*. Printed in bold letters or in italics, headings suggest the kind of material you will find in a small portion of the reading.
- **Look at the pictures, charts, or drawings.**
  Often an illustration and a caption can help you figure out beforehand what your reading will deal with.
- **Look at the first paragraph carefully.**
  The first paragraph usually tells what the reading will be about. Read it; then stop to absorb the information before reading more.
- **Look at the first sentence of each paragraph.**
  This gives you a quick idea of what the reading involves, before you begin to read carefully.

- **Look at the questions that come after the reading.**
  Look at the questions *before* you read to determine what to expect from a passage and what kind of information to look for.
- **Look for key words in different print.**
  Sometimes bold letters, italics, or even colored ink call the reader's attention to important words or ideas.
- **Look for a summary.**
  At the end of a long factual piece, a writer sometimes summarizes the main points. Looking at this summary before you read can help you grasp more clearly what the section deals with.

Note how elements in this selection from an economics book help you preview the piece to determine its content and focus.

STUDY QUESTION
↘
What is economics?

The Definition of Economics

People want more *goods* and *services* than they have or can purchase with their incomes. Whether they are wealthy or poor, what they have is never enough. Neither the poor nor the wealthy have unlimited resources. Both have only so much income and time, and both must make choices to allocate these limited resources in ways that best satisfy their wants.

WORD DEFINITIONS IN MARGIN
↘

scarcity the shortage that exists when less of something is available than is wanted at a zero price

Because wants are unlimited and incomes, goods, time, and other items are not, scarcity exists everywhere. **Scarcity** exists when people want more of an item than is available when the price of the item is zero.

Scarcity means that at a zero price the quantity of a good or resource is not sufficient to satisfy people's unlimited wants. Any good for which this holds is called an **economic good.** If there is enough of a good available at

economic good any good that is scarce

Each time you purchase a compact disk (CD), even on sale for $11.99, you give up whatever else that $11.99 could purchase. For $11.99 you could have a pizza and two soft drinks; you could purchase two novels; you could see two movies; you could purchase a ticket to one concert; or you could buy one tank of gas. You must make a choice. You can't have everything you want because resources are scarce; your income is limited. If you buy the CD, you have determined that it provides you more enjoyment for that $11.99 than any other use of the money.

free good　a good for which there is no scarcity
bad　any item for which we would pay to have less

a zero price to satisfy wants, the good is said to be a **free good.** If people would pay to have less of a good, that good is called a **bad.** It is difficult to think of examples of free goods. At one time people referred to air as free, but with air pollution so prevalent, it is difficult to consider air a free good. It is not so hard to think of examples of bads: pollution, garbage, and disease fit the description.

Because people's wants are unlimited and the things they want and the income they have are scarce, individuals must make choices. But when they choose some things, they must give up or forgo other things. Economics is the study of how people choose to use their scarce resources to attempt to satisfy their **unlimited wants.**

unlimited wants
boundless desires for goods and services

The choices people make are those they believe to be in their self-interest—that is, they believe they will receive more satisfaction from their choice than they would receive if they selected something else. **Rational self-interest** is the term economists use to describe how people make choices. It means that people will make the choices that, at the time and with the information they have at their disposal, will give them the greatest amount of satisfaction.

What is rational self-interest?

rational self-interest
the term economists use to describe how people make choices

As illustrated in Figure 1, there are four categories of resources used to produce goods and services: land, labor, capital, and entrepreneurial ability. **Land** includes all natural resources, such as minerals, timber, and water, as well as the land itself. **Labor** refers to the physical and intellectual services of people and includes the training, education, and abilities of the individuals in a society.

land   all natural resources, such as minerals, timber, and water, as well as the land itself.

labor   the physical and intellectual services of people, including the training, education, and abilities of the individuals in a society

Capital refers to products such as machinery and equipment that are used in production. Capital is a manufactured or created product used solely to produce goods and services. For example, tractors, milling machines, and cotton gins are capital; automobiles and food are goods; and haircuts and manicures are services. The word *capital* is often used to describe financial backing or the dollars used to finance a business. *Financial capital* refers to the money value of capital, as represented by stocks and bonds. In economics, *capital* refers to a physical entity—machinery and equipment and offices, warehouses, and factories.

capital   products such as machinery and equipment that are used in production

entrepreneurial ability
the ability to recognize a profitable opportunity and the willingness and ability to organize land, labor, and capital and assume the risk associated with the opportunity

Entrepreneurial ability is the ability to recognize a profitable opportunity and

Figure 1
Four Categories of Resources

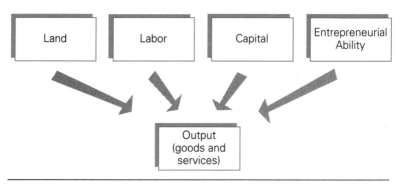

the willingness and ability to organize land, labor, and capital and assume the risk associated with the opportunity. A special talent that only a few individuals have, entrepreneurial ability plays such an important role in the economy that it is considered to be a separate resource rather than just an aspect of labor. People who demonstrate entrepreneurial abilities are called **entrepreneurs**. . . .

entrepreneur an individual who has the ability to organize resources in order to produce a product and the willingness to take the risk to pursue a profitable opportunity.

Recap

SUMMARY →

1. Economics is the study of how people choose to use their scarce resources to satisfy their unlimited wants.
2. Resources are classified into four general groups: land, labor, capital, and entrepreneurial ability.
3. Scarce resources are used to produce goods and services.

— William Boyes and Michael Melvin

2e   Preview the Parts of a Book

Before you read a book for information (as opposed to reading a chapter or a selection), you can use some other effective preview techniques aside from those explained in section **2a.** Here is how to preview a book:

- **Look at the table of contents.**
  Found at the front of the book, the table of contents lists chapter and section titles and the pages on which chapters begin. If you study the chapter titles, you can get an idea of what each part of the book deals with and how the topics relate to one another.
- **Look at the preface.**
  Also located at the front of the book, the preface (or *foreword*) is a personal message to the reader. In the preface you get an idea of the kind of reader the author is writing for; of the aims of the book and just what the author expects you to learn as a result of reading it; and of the topics in the book and the best approaches to those topics.
- **Look briefly at the index.**
  At the end of a book, you may find an index, which is an alphabetical listing of the topics, subjects, ideas, and names mentioned in the book. A quick look at the index suggests some of the points the writer deals with and how detailed the book is.
- **Look at one of these special features that sometimes appear in books:**

1. A *glossary* sometimes appears after the chapters in a book. The glossary consists of a list of difficult words or terms commonly used in the subject the book deals with. The words are listed in alphabetical order along with their definitions.
2. An *appendix* (plural *appendixes* or *appendices*) at the end of the book presents additional informa-

tion, such as charts and graphs, special letters or documents, or facts about the lives of the people mentioned in the book.

- **Read the introduction.**
  Often a first chapter, the introduction gives an overview of the book and states the basic problem the author will deal with. It gives background information or discusses the history of the topic. It may summarize what others have said about the subject. It may even explain the method of research the author used. Sometimes—especially for a work of fiction (a novel, a collection of short stories, a play)—someone other than the author writes the introduction.

- **Look at the bibliography or references.**
  At the back of the book, an author sometimes gives a *bibliography*—a list, in alphabetical order, of some or all of the books that helped the author write the book. The bibliography (or works cited list) indicates the author's range of knowledge and basic interests.

- **Think about what parts the book has and what parts it doesn't have.**
  A book with a detailed index, a long bibliography, and a number of appendixes may be more appropriate for research than a book with only a short table of contents. And books with glossaries often provide helpful introductions to difficult subjects.

Read the table of contents from the book *Contemporary Business Communication* by Scot Ober on page 24 to learn as much as possible about the content of the book.

What information does the preface on page 25 give you about the book *Good Dirt: Confessions of a Conservationist* by David E. Morine?

Look at the excerpt from the index for *Contemporary Business Communication* on page 26 to determine

BRIEF CONTENTS

Sample Table of Contents

PREFACE

Conservation is my chosen profession. From 1972 to 1987 I was in charge of land acquisition for The Nature Conservancy, a nonprofit organization. During that time, we acquired three million acres of land, completed 5,000 projects, and protected 2,000 of America's most significant natural areas. We ran a good business. We raised some money. We saved some land. We had some fun.

When I started with the Conservancy, saving land was a relatively simple business. We'd look around, find some land that we liked, and buy it. Once we had acquired an area, I really believed that it would be protected in perpetuity. I, like most people, had never heard of acid rain, the greenhouse effect, or holes in the ozone layer. We didn't deal in doom and gloom. We bought land.

Today, things are different. Dire predictions seem to be the staple of the conservation movement. Most conservationists are consumed by problems for which there are no simple solutions. What good does it do, for example, to buy a forest unless you can protect if from acid rain? Why save a tidal marsh if it is going to be lost to rising oceans resulting from global warming? Who can worry about a piece of native tallgrass prairie when we are destroying the atmosphere? It is no wonder that so many of today's conservationists seem so somber. They see so many threats to the environment that they can't enjoy being conservationists. For them, humor has become a rare and endangered species.

During my tenure at The Nature Conservancy, we were generally considered to be the most businesslike of the conservation organizations. We probably were. But that didn't mean that we didn't have our share of screwups. Any time you undertake a major land deal, something is going to go wrong. When that happens, you can do one of two things: You can get upset, or you can laugh. More often than not, we laughed.

I believe that a large part of the Conservancy's success has been due to the fact that we never took ourselves too seriously. We never let the big issues get us down. We never spent too much time agonizing over the big picture. We attacked the problem of saving significant natural areas one piece at a time.

We weren't naive. We knew we weren't going to save the world, but we thought we could save small and important parts of it. We were focused in our work; we were happy being conservationists.

This collection of stories describes some of my more monumental foulups. Most are informative; a few are irreverent, and at least one is totally tasteless. Despite my having been justifiably accused of never letting the facts get in the way of a good story, these stories are, on the whole, true. I hope they will explain a little about land conservation and give conservationists a much-needed lift. With all the doom and gloom being written today, we could use a laugh.

what additional information you can find about the topics that are covered in the book.

APPLICATIONS: Your Courses

Select a textbook that you are using in one of your courses. Locate the following parts of the book: table of contents, preface, index, special features. Consider the information each part gives you about the book.

2f Understand Types of Textbooks

Textbooks differ not only in their subject but in the very thing they ask you to do with the subject.

Some textbooks simply present the information that you need to memorize, as when an anatomy book names bones you must learn. Some textbooks present many facts that you need to put together to create a larger picture, such as historical forces and movements in a history textbook.

Other textbooks provide problems to solve and instructions for the solution, as in a math textbook.

Still others provide general principles and examples to help you think through real-life situations, as in many management textbooks.

Finally, some textbooks present a series of historical documents, poems and stories, or critical arguments for you to read, interpret, and discuss.

Each kind of textbook requires a particular type of work as you read it. Understanding what the major kinds of textbooks are like will improve the way you read them.

2f(1) *Skill-Building Textbooks*

To help you master new skills, many textbooks list and explain the rules, concepts, and procedures associated with each skill and then provide examples and problems for practice. Many math, language, and communication textbooks are skill-building, as are books for specific careers, like accountancy or law.

Skill Exercise 8.1 *Responsive Listening*

Responsive listening involves listening to understand what the other person is saying from his or her perspective. For each of the messages listed below, indicate how you would typically respond and how you might respond using responsive listening.

1. Jim says, "I got a D on my exam in interpersonal communication. I have to get a C for the course to count toward my general education credit."

   How would you typically respond? _____

   How would you respond to Jim using responsive listening?

   _____

   _____

2. Sue says, "I don't think that my boss likes me. I don't know how to approach the boss to talk about it."

   How would you typically respond? _____

   How would you respond to Sue using responsive listening?

   _____

   _____

3. Lisa says, "I just heard that the guy I've been dating is seeing someone else. I don't know what to do."

   How would you typically respond? _____

   How would you respond to Lisa using responsive listening?

   _____

   _____

— William Gudykunst et al.

To get the most out of these books, you must do more than merely read the rules and guidelines. You have to use those rules and guidelines to carry out tasks and solve problems, such as the kind provided in the exercises. In most cases, the exercises will help you discover solutions and procedures on your own. To learn the skills effectively, you must take an active approach to working the exercises that reinforce them.

The passage on page 28 from a communications textbook offers only one paragraph of instruction on responsive listening. Then it provides exercises requiring you to apply the skill in some real-world situations.

2f(2) *Textbooks for Information*

Although all textbooks present information, some introduce many facts and connect them in a big picture. Such textbooks often have charts, graphs, illustrations, and sidebars that allow the writers to present additional facts and statistics related to the subject matter. Furthermore, these texts often have overviews at the beginning of each chapter or unit to give a context for the readings. Summaries at the end often state the most important points covered.

You should read all such text materials carefully and think of how the facts fit together into a larger framework. Pay special attention to sidebars, overviews, summaries, charts, words, and phrases in boldface or italics, and concepts defined in the margins.

You should aim at becoming able to retell the information you have read about, both the details and the larger issues. Exams in courses that use such books will typically ask you to remember facts through short-answer questions and re-create the big picture through essay questions.

In the following example from a history textbook, the author weaves facts about the Berlin airlift into a larger picture that includes the political objectives of both the United States and the Soviet Union.

7 Faced with the prospect of a pro-Western, industrialized, and eventually remilitarized Germany, Stalin reacted. On April 1, 1948, after asking for a Four Powers meeting to discuss Germany, the Soviets briefly denied entry from the West to the city of Berlin—the old German capital, which lay entirely within the Soviet occupational zone and which also was divided into zones controlled by the Four Powers. On June 23, ignoring Soviet objections, officials issued the new currency in the western zones of Berlin. The following day, the Russians blockaded all land traffic to and from Berlin and shut off the electricity to the city's western zones. With a population of over 2 million, West Berlin lay isolated 120 miles inside the Soviet zone of Germany. The Soviet goal was to force the West either to abandon the creation of West Germany or to face the loss of Berlin. Americans viewed the blockade simply as further proof of Soviet hostility and were determined not to retreat. Churchill affirmed the West's stand. We want peace, he stated, "but we should by now have learned that there is no safety in yielding to dictators, whether Nazi or Communist." The prospect of war loomed.

Having decided to stay in Berlin, American strategists confronted the question of how to stand fast without starting a shooting war. Although some in the army recommended fighting their way across the Soviet zone to the city, Truman chose another option, one that would not violate Soviet occupied territory or any international agreements. In November 1945, the Allies, including the Soviet Union, had agreed to maintain three air corridors to Berlin from the West, providing no legal right for Soviet interference with air traffic. Marshalling a massive effort of men, supplies, and aircraft, British and Americans flew through these corridors to three Berlin airports on an average of one flight every three minutes. To drive home to the Soviets the depth of American resolve, Truman ordered a wing of B-29 bombers, the "atomic bombers," to Berlin. Although these planes carried no atomic weapons, the general impression was that their presence deterred the likelihood of Soviet aggression.

The **Berlin airlift** was a tremendous victory for the United States. . . .

— *Carol Berkin et al.*

2f(3) *Concept-Building Textbooks*

Many textbooks explain theories and conceptual frameworks that people in their disciplines use to understand facts and detailed information.

Textbooks concerned with concepts usually ask you to do more than just memorize; you need to understand the concepts behind the facts and be able to apply these concepts to situations that are not specifically covered in the text. Such books offer numerous extended examples of the concepts, often placed in sidebars. Questions at the end of each section or chapter often help you apply the concepts.

The following passage from a government textbook proposes a new conceptual framework to replace the traditional labels "liberal" and "conservative." Think of how the new categories would apply to political opinions that are not described in the text.

 Ideological Types in the United States

Our ideological typology in Chapter 1 classifies people as liberals if they favor freedom over order and equality over freedom. Conversely, conservatives favor freedom over equality and order over freedom. Libertarians favor freedom over both equality and order—the opposite of populists. By cross-tabulating people's answers to the two questions about freedom versus order (abortion) and freedom versus equality (government job guarantees), we can classify respondents according to their ideological tendencies. As

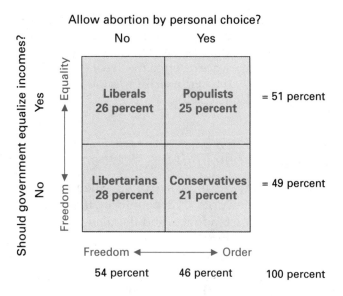

Figure 5.5 Two survey questions presented choices between freedom and order and between freedom and equality by asking respondents whether abortion should be a matter of personal choice or of government regulation, and whether government should guarantee a job and good standard of living or people should get ahead on their own . . . . People's responses to the questions showed no correlation, demonstrating that these value choices cannot be explained by a simple liberal-conservative continuum. Instead, their responses can be more usefully analyzed according to four different ideological types. (The one-point difference in the percentage of responses for the "government guarantee jobs" question from that given on page 158 is the result of losing a few cases when the questions are cross tabulated.) (Source: 1992 National Election Study, Center for Political Studies, University of Michigan.)

shown in Figure 5.5, people's responses to the two questions are virtually unrelated—that is, the responses fall about equally within each of the quadrants. This finding indicates that people do not decide about government activity according to a one-dimensional ideological standard. Figure 5.5 also classifies the sample according to the two dimensions in our ideological typology. Using only two issues to classify people in an ideological framework leaves substantial room for error. Still, if the typology is worthwhile, the results should be meaningful, and they are.

It is striking that the ideological tendencies of the respondents in the 1992 sample depicted in Figure 5.5 are divided almost equally among the four categories of the typology. (Remember, however, that these categories—like letter grades A, B, C, and D—are more rigid in the typology that in the respondents. Many would cluster toward the center of the figure, if their attitudes were measured more sensitively.) The populist response pattern is the most common by a small margin and the libertarian the least common. The sample suggests that more than three-quarters of the electorate favor government action to promote order, increase equality, or both. The results resemble earlier findings by other researchers who conducted more exhaustive analyses involving more survey questions.

Respondents who readily locate themselves on a single dimension running from liberal to conservative often go on to contradict their self-placement when answering questions that trade freedom for either order or equality. A two-dimensional typology such as that in Figure 5.5 allows us to analyze responses more meaningfully. A slight majority of respondents (52 percent) expresses opinions that are either liberal (26 percent) or conservative (26 percent), but almost as many express opinions that deviate from these familiar ideological types.

— *Kenneth Janda et al.*

2f(4) *Applied Textbooks*

Many textbooks focus on showing how general principles apply to real-world situations. This approach is especially common to textbooks designed to prepare you to enter a specific career or discipline, such as management or social work.

When you read an application-oriented textbook, you should try to imagine yourself in the situations described. Try to think beyond the specific situations presented in the text, perhaps to situations you have already experienced on a job or in some other setting.

The following selection from a business textbook applies the general principles of human resource development to the difficult question of romance in the workplace.

 ### Getting Ahead in Business

Romance in the Workplace:
Should You Get Involved?

With more women in the workplace and members of both sexes functioning closely together, blossoming romances seem unavoidable. After all, work is a likely place to meet someone with similar interests and goals. In a study done by a *Fortune* 500 consultant, seventy-six out of one hundred women surveyed said they had recently witnessed an office romance or had been involved in one. However, problems connected with office romances, whether between employer and employee or coworkers, often have negative effects on workplace morale, motivation, and productivity.

A recent study distinguishes three categories of office romance, suggesting that some types offer more potential for harm than others.

- *True Love:*   Regarded as genuine and long-term.
  Coworkers don't usually object.
  Few problems arise if this situation is properly managed.
- *The Fling:*   Characterized as intensely passionate and exciting.
  Short-lived.
  Coworkers tend to frown on this one.
- *Utilitarian:*   One partner trades sex for career advancement.
  Most harmful relationship.

> Most commonly (62 percent according to a recent survey) occurs between a woman and a man in a higher-level position.

In the workplace, managers are expected to deal with employees fairly, and coworkers must treat each other with mutual respect. When exploitation undermines this foundation, productivity and careers can crumble. Management can take an active role in preventing romance (or sex) from upsetting the work environment, but attitudes and policies vary. A *Business Week* survey reveals that most companies' written policies stipulate only that married couples may not work for or with each other. Years ago, anthropologist Margaret Mead advised that sexual involvement at work must be taboo if men and women are to work together effectively. Today, many businesses argue that freedom and individual rights justify allowing workers to engage in office romances, and a recent Gallup poll indicates that more than half of working Americans find workplace dating acceptable. Management experts have developed some useful guidelines, based on the view that management should respond to office relationships only when the potential for a severe offense exists or when it is certain that an offense has been committed.

— William Pride, Robert Hughes, and Jack Kapoor

2f(5) *Anthologies*

Some textbooks collect readings from other sources into an *anthology*. Literature classes, for example, often use anthologies of stories, poems, or plays. Philosophy classes often use anthologies of passages from major philosophic works. History classes often assign collections of historical documents that give samples of what people of the period did, said, and thought.

Anthology editions usually offer more than just collections of other people's work, by providing information and cues for interpretation that can help you more fully understand the selections. Look for the following features when you examine an anthology:

- An introduction that sets forth some of the common themes that connect all the readings.
- Headnotes that give background information about the text.
- Biographical information about the author.
- Footnotes that explain difficult words and concepts.
- Glossaries of key terms.
- Questions at the end of each reading to help you think through important issues.

Look at the following selection from a literature anthology. Consider how the different material that surrounds the poem helps you understand the poem better.

Frank O'Hara

Born in Baltimore, Maryland, and educated at Harvard, Frank O'Hara (1926–1966) was associated with a group of artists and writers known as the New York School. O'Hara himself worked as an assistant curator at the Museum of Modern Art in New York, and his poetry demonstrates a clear affinity with the visual arts. Both his early death from a car accident and the quality of "camp" (that is, a combination of the whimsical, inconsequential, witty, and delightful) in his poetry have added to his mystique. His poems, however, stand on their own. His reputation was established with the posthumous publication of The Collected Poems of Frank O'Hara *(1971). His poems, expressing personal emotions, impressions, and variations, have the persuasiveness of immediacy. Often colloquial and witty, they evade form and avoid easy intellectual statements.*

Why I Am Not a Painter

I am not a painter, I am a poet.
  Why? I think I would rather be
a painter, but I am not. Well,

For instance, Mike Goldberg
  is starting a painting I drop in.   5
"Sit down and have a drink," he
  says. I drink; we drink. I look
up. "You have SARDINES in it."
  "Yes, it needed something there."
"Oh." I go and the days go by   10
  and I drop in again. The painting
is going on, and I go, and the days
  go by. I drop in. The painting is
finished. "Where's SARDINES?"
  All that's left is just   15
letters, "It was too much," Mike says.

But me? One day I am thinking of
  a color: orange. I write a line
about orange. Pretty soon it is a
  whole page or words, not lines.   20
Then another page. There should be
  so much more, not of orange, of
words, of how terrible orange is
  and life. Days go by. It is even in
prose, I am a real poet. My poem   25
  is finished and I haven't mentioned
orange yet. It's twelve poems, I call
  it ORANGES. And one day in a gallery
I see Mike's painting, called SARDINES.

Study Questions

1. According to "Why I Am Not a Painter," how does a painting like that by Mike Goldberg evolve? Are the explanations the painter gives for why he does what he does rational?

2. The poem's title suggests that painting and poetry are different art forms. Does the poet support this suggestion? In what ways are painting a picture

and writing a poem different and in what ways similar?

3. The poem works through humor and irony. Analyze the effects of lines such as "[the poem] is even in /prose, I am a real poet."

— *Shirley Lim and Norman Spencer*

Types of Textbooks

Skill-Building Textbooks

Aim: to help you master new skills

Typical features: rules and procedures; examples and problems

Often used in: math, language, physics and chemistry, communication, economics, accounting

Tips: Use procedures to carry out tasks and solve problems.

Textbooks for Information

Aim: to present facts and connect them in a big picture

Typical features: charts, graphs, illustrations, sidebars, overviews, and summaries

Often used in: history, biology, astronomy

Tips: Read all of the materials carefully and think of how the facts fit together into a larger framework. Pay special attention to facts and concepts in boldface or italics.

Concept-Building Textbooks

Aim: to help you make sense out of the facts you learn

Typical features: descriptions of theories and conceptual frameworks, examples and illustrations

Often used in: sociology, psychology, anthropology, philosophy
Tips: Pay attention to understanding concepts.

Applied Textbooks

Aim: to help you apply principles to real-world situations
Typical features: rules and procedures; examples and problems
Often used in: business, management, social work
Tips: Imagine yourself in the situations described; think about decisions you would have to make.

Anthologies

Aim: to provide selections to read and discuss
Typical features: selections, introductions and headnotes, background information, footnotes and glossaries
Often used in: literature, philosophy, history
Tips: Use the support tools to help yourself understand the selections.

 APPLICATIONS: Your Courses

Choose three textbooks from your courses. Identify the type of textbook each one is. Then describe what each book asks you to do and which features of that book help you with the task.

3

Visual Aids

Photographs, drawings, graphs, tables, charts, maps, and diagrams often add to the meaning of a text. Often a *caption*—that is, a brief explanation in words—accompanies the visual aid and highlights its most important elements.

Each visual carries a message in itself, but the message also connects with the ideas and information in the main text.

Sometimes a photo or diagram simply illustrates or reinforces a point made in the writing. A newspaper article describing a meeting between the leaders of the United States and France may include a photo of them shaking hands and smiling.

In other cases, visuals add new but related information that helps enrich your understanding of the text itself. (See pages 18–21.)

Sometimes an essential part of the reading is visual in nature and is best represented in an illustration. Then the illustration works hand in hand with the words. (See pages 41–44.)

Finally, the visual aid may be the most important part of the selection, and the words only help explain the picture. (See page 45.)

3a Photographs and Drawings

To interpret photographs and drawings, first identify what is being represented; then try to infer moods, attitudes, and relations that help give life to the pictures, particularly when they are of people.

Thoughtful readers who pause over photographs and drawings often ask themselves a number of questions. These questions can help connect the visual aid with the written information that goes with it.

Questions for Understanding Photographs and Drawings

- What is the scene of the photograph or drawing and how does it relate to the point in the reading selection?
- Who is the person in the picture and what is the person doing?
- What is the relation among the various people in the picture? Why are these people (or this person) at the scene?
- What moods can I identify from the people's faces or gestures? How do I interpret—that is, explain—people's behavior?
- How does the caption relate to the photograph or drawing? What information is missing from the caption? How can I explain the information that is missing?
- What was the picture included with the written selection?

In the selection that follows, although the caption explains the pictures, and the pictures make the visual point very well, you must connect the words in the selection with the visual aids.

  Depth Perception

Thanks to the constancies of perception, people perceive coherent, stable objects. Imagine trying to deal

Figure 1 A Violation of Size Constancy   The two baseball players in the picture appear to be of very different size, even though you know that their heights are probably much the same. The discussion of stimulus cues to depth explains why.

with a world in which objects changed their form as often as their images changed on your retinas. But Figure 1 shows a case in which perceptual constancy fails. Why does the nearer baseball player seem larger? Why does size constancy fail here?

The answer lies in the perceived distance, one of the most important factors underlying size and shape constancy. Perception of distance, or **depth perception,** allows people to experience the world in three-dimensional depth. How can this occur, when all visual information comes through a set of two-dimensional retinas? There are two reasons: cues provided by the environment, sometimes described as *stimulus cues,* and properties of the visual system itself.

To some extent, people perceive depth through the same cues that artists use to create the impression of depth and distance on a two-dimensional canvas.

Figure 2 Stimulus Cues for Depth Perception   See if you can identify how cues of relative size, interposition, linear perspective, height in the visual field, textural gradient, and shadows combine to create a sense of three-dimensionality.

These cues are actually characteristics of visual stimuli and therefore illustrate the ecological view of perception. Figure 2 demonstrates several of these cues.

- Look first at the two men at the far left of Figure 2. They illustrate the principle of **relative size:** if two objects are assumed to be the same size, the object producing a larger image on the retina is perceived as closer than the one producing a smaller image.
- Another cue comes from **height in the visual field:** on the ground, more distant objects are usually higher in the visual field than those nearby. The woman near the man at the front of Figure 2 therefore appears to be farther away.
- The woman walking by the car in the middle of Figure 2 illustrates another depth cue called **interposition,** or *occlusion.* Closer objects block the view

of things farther away. Because of misleading cues from both height in the visual field and interposition, size constancy was violated in Figure 1. The more distant ballplayer is lower, not higher in the visual field; also the runner's leg appears to be in front of, not behind the pitcher's leg, thereby providing a misleading interposition cue. Together, these misleading cues make the runner appear smaller than normal rather then farther away.

- The figure at the far right of Figure 2 is seen as still farther away, in part because she is standing near a point in the road where its edges, like all parallel lines that recede into the distance, appear to converge toward a single point. This apparent convergence provides a cue called **linear perspective.** The closer together two converging lines are, the greater the perceived distance.

- Notice that the road in the picture disappears into a hazy background. Since greater distances usually produce less clarity, **reduced clarity** is interpreted as a cue for greater distance. The effect of clarity on perceived distance explains why a mountain viewed on a hazy day appears to loom larger than the same mountain on a clear day. The haze acts as a cue for greater distance, but the size of the mountain's retinal image is unchanged. The same retinal image accompanied by a greater perceived distance produces a larger perceived size.

- **Light and shadow** also contribute to the perception of three dimensions (Ramachandran, 1988). The buildings in the background of Figure 2 are seen as three-dimensional cubes, not flat billboards, because of the shadows on their right faces.

— *Douglas A. Bernstein et al.*

3b   Diagrams

A diagram is a drawing with labeled parts. Labels and captions usually point out key features and explain how the parts relate to one another. In the illustration below, labels and a caption in a science textbook work along with the diagram to explain how fraternal and identical twins are formed.

3c Word Charts

A word chart presents information in summary form to make material easy to find. Instead of using sen-

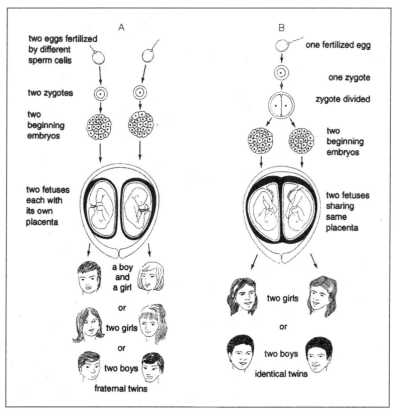

Forming Twins   (A) Fraternal twins develop from two fertilized eggs.
(B) Identical twins develop from one fertilized egg.

tences in a paragraph, a writer can present complex information in chart form. This textbook uses word charts regularly: See pages 7–8 and 38–39, for example.

In the word chart on page 47, notice how the visual layout makes it easy to understand the examples of punctuation.

3d   Statistical Tables

Statistical tables present numbers in chart form. Often the numbers appear in columns with headings to explain what the numbers represent. Titles also point out important information. Compare the numbers with one another and with what you expect from the numbers, in order to find meanings.

In the statistical table on page 48, note how the title and subtitle explain the purpose of the table: to provide an AIDS report that shows the number of HIV and AIDS cases worldwide. Each numbered heading names a geographical region; other headings identify what the figures mean.

3e   Graphs

Graphs present statistics visually and show how statistics compare with one another. When you look at a statistical table, you have to make comparisons on your own; in a graph, the size or shape of the drawing helps you make the comparison. In reading graphs, study the title and labels carefully.

Notice how the bar graph on page 49 about immigrants allows you to see relations among numbers. For example, the bar for 1931–1940 is much smaller than the bar directly above it, for 1921–1930. This visual comparison tells you that fewer immigrants

A Handy Punctuation Chart

MARK	EXPLANATION AND EXAMPLES
•	To end sentences and abbreviations: Dr. Smith called.
?	To end direct questions: What time is it?
!	To show surprise or strong emotion: I don't believe it!
,	To separate words, phrases, and sentences in a series: apples, oranges, pineapples, and bananas To separate words and phrases not part of the main idea of a sentence: Fran, *the teacher's pet*, got all the answers right. To use in titles, dates, addresses: Allen Schwartz, M.D. June 30, 1945 Elk, California
—	To interrupt a sentence and to emphasize added-in phrases: Phil—*our last hope*—came to bat.
( )	To separate interrupting material: Candy Jones (*of the prominent Jones family*) invited me to a party.
[ ]	To add your own words in a quotation: "Four score [*that means eighty*] and seven years ago . . ."

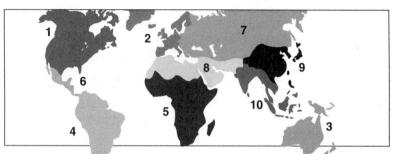

An AIDS Report

1. North America

	HIV	AIDS
Total Cases:	1,138,000	327,000
Men:	963,000	276,000
Women:	160,000	46,000
Children*:	14,000	5,000

2. Western Europe

	HIV	AIDS
Total Cases:	660,000	124,000
Men:	545,000	102,000
Women:	109,000	20,000
Children*:	8,000	2,000

3. Oceania

	HIV	AIDS
Total Cases:	27,000	6,000
Men:	24,000	5,000
Women:	3,000	Less than 1,000
Children*:	Less than 1,000	Less than 1,000

4. Latin America

	HIV	AIDS
Total Cases:	1,313,000	400,000
Men:	1,002,000	283,000
Women:	250,000	71,000
Children*:	61,000	46,000

5. Sub-Saharan Africa

	HIV	AIDS
Total Cases:	15,459,000	5,770,000
Men:	6,411,000	2,051,000
Women:	7,052,000	2,258,000
Children*:	1,996,000	1,463,000

The number of HIV and AIDS cases worldwide as of Jan. 1, 1994

SOURCE: Global AIDS Policy Coalition

*HIV infection acquired before or at birth

6. Caribbean

	HIV	AIDS
Total Cases:	402,000	103,000
Men:	225,000	50,000
Women:	150,000	33,000
Children*:	26,000	9,000

7. Eastern Europe

	HIV	AIDS
Total Cases:	28,000	5,000
Men:	25,000	5,000
Women:	3,000	Less than 1,000
Children*:	1,000	Less than 1,000

8. Southeastern Mediterranean

	HIV	AIDS
Total Cases:	58,000	8,000
Men:	47,000	6,000
Women:	9,000	1,000
Children*:	2,000	Less than 1,000

9. Northeast Asia

	HIV	AIDS
Total Cases:	94,000	4,000
Men:	77,000	3,000
Women:	15,000	Less than 1,000
Children*:	1,000	Less than 1,000

10. Southeast Asia

	HIV	AIDS
Total Cases:	3,020,000	95,000
Men:	1,968,000	42,000
Women:	984,000	21,000
Children*:	68,000	32,000

World Totals

	HIV	AIDS
Total Cases:	22,200,000	6,842,000
Men:	11,287,000	2,825,000
Women:	8,737,000	2,451,000
Children*:	2,175,000	1,566,000

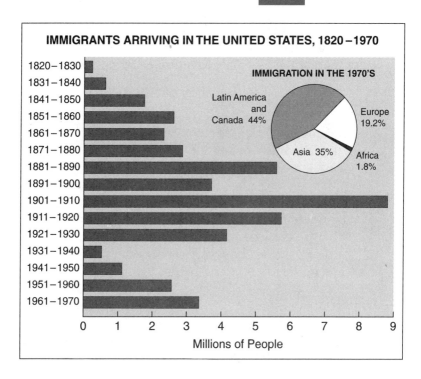

came to the United States in the 1930s than in the 1920s. In the circle graph about immigration in the 1970s, notice the small piece for African immigrants. Even if you didn't read the low percentage of African immigrants—1.8 percent—you could tell from the drawing that the number of African immigrants was small in relation to others.

3f   Maps

Maps point out geographical, historical, or scientific issues, among others. A history book will display migration patterns across the country during the expansion of America's West. A geology book will present maps to indicate weather patterns. A geography book will show the changing boundaries of European or African countries. An astronomy book will provide a map of the night sky to indicate star patterns.

How to Read a Map

- **Examine the captions and titles carefully.** The various labels will identify the areas and regions under consideration and will tell you the general focus of the map. Make sure that you understand what the map is attempting to present.
- **Examine the legend.** Usually a *legend*—an explanation of the various colors, marks, or symbols used in the map—accompanies the map itself. You need to refer to the legend to understand the visual presentation. (Why do certain countries or regions appear in a particular color or pattern?)
- **Be sure that you understand the scale.** A *scale* helps you determine the actual distance from one place on the map to another. An inch on the map may represent 100 miles or 200 kilometers; using a ruler, you can estimate distances and sizes so that relations among the various elements on the map are clear.

In the example on page 51 from an American history text, the map title "The States Choose Sides" from a chapter on the Civil War tells you the purpose of the map. Note how the legend at the bottom explains the different visual patterns. The areas with dark shading indicate the Confederate states. The clear areas indicate the Union States. The states with light shading indicate the border states not seceding.

The map provides the names of the states. You can see easily which states belong in each group. But as an active reader, you should raise a number of questions. For example, why has the writer included the map in the first place? How many states belong in each group? Why did some states define themselves as "border" and not secede? What special problems might border states have faced? Why did the Confederacy claim certain states in federally controlled territories? Why did California and Oregon, far away from the conflict, define themselves as Union states?

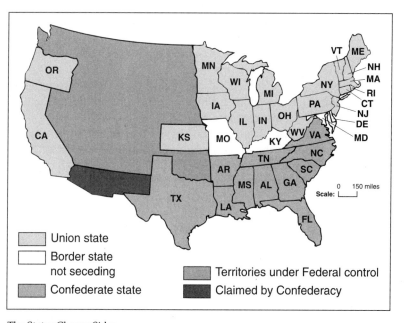

The States Choose Sides

3g   Words and Visuals Together

Often graphs, tables, and illustrations accompany text in order to help make the writer's point, as in the selection on page 52 about people's religious identification. To understand the writer's point, you have to use both the visual information and the written paragraphs.

Practicing or Not,
Many Identify with Religion

Most Americans are religious and aren't afraid to say so, a sweeping new survey on religious affiliation shows.

The survey, commissioned by the Graduate School of the City University of New York, found 86.5% of Americans identified themselves as Christians, 2% as Jewish and 0.5% as Muslim.

Only 7.5% of the respondents said they had no religion.

But a closer look at the data shows striking diversity. Of the Christians, 26% said they were Roman Catholic and 60% said Protestant. And respondents identified with more than 50 denominations, including Taoist and Hindu.

"The tremendous diversity of denominations shows the cross-cutting cohesive tendency of religion," says study director Barry Kosmin. "All of these groups cut across racial, ethnic, class, regional and generational lines."

The survey—of 113,000 people across the USA interviewed during a period of 13 months—is the largest and most comprehensive poll to date on religious affiliation. It was conducted because the USA "did not have a good religious profile," says Seymour Lachman, dean of community development at City University.

Despite concern that some people might be offended by questions about their religion, few refused to answer the poll. "It demonstrates that for many Americans, religious identity is important, perhaps as important as their ethnic or racial identity," says Lachman.

Other findings:

- The greatest percentage of respondents who have no religion live in the West; Oregon has the highest with 17%.

—Julie Stacey

USA Remains Solidly Religious

Overall

Christian
86.5%

No Religion
7.5%

Non-Christian
3.7%

Refused to answer
2.3%

Pentecostals have lowest median age, Presbyterians are oldest

	Median Age
Presbyterian	48.2
Methodist	48.0
Episcopalian	45.7
Lutheran	45.4
Jewish	44.4
Baptist	44.1
Mormon	41.6
Catholic	40.1
Pentecostal	39.8

Jewish are most urban, Baptists the least

Jewish	96%
Catholic	84.5%
Episcopalian	83.3%
Presbyterian	77.8%
Mormon	72.9%
Lutheran	71.2%
Pentecostal	69%
Methodist	66.3%
Baptist	66.1%

Top 5 states with percentages of adherents that exceed the national average:

Baptist — Nat. avg.: 19%
D.C. 37%, N.C. 47%, Ga. 51%, Miss. 55%, Ala. 51%

Jewish — Nat. avg.: 2%
Ma. 4%, N.J. 4%, Md. 3%, N.Y. 7%, Fla. 4%

Methodist — Nat. avg.: 8%
W. Va. 15%, Iowa 16%, Kan. 15%, Del. 27%, S.C. 18%

No religion — Nat. avg.: 7.5%
Wash. 14%, Ore. 17%, Calif. 13%, Wyo. 14%, Ariz. 12%

Catholic — Nat. avg.: 26%
Mass. 54%, R.I. 62%, Conn. 50%, N.J. 46%, La. 47%

Lutheran — Nat. avg.: 5%
Minn. 34%, N.D. 37%, S.D. 30%, Neb. 18%, Wis. 26%

Source: Telephone survey of 113,000 households in the 48 contiguous states from April 1989 – April 1990 by ICR Survey Research Group of Media, Pa., for the Graduate School and University Center of the City University of New York; sampling error: 1%

- Half of all black U.S. residents are Baptist, 9% are Catholic.
- Hispanics make up 14% of all Catholics, and 65% of Hispanics are Catholic.
- Most Irish-Americans are Protestant, exploding the belief that most are Catholic.
- Most Asian-Americans and Arab-Americans are Christians.
- Mormons have the highest proportion of married adults and the most children.
- Greek Orthodox members have the lowest rate of divorce and Unitarians the highest.
- The major churches remain Roman Catholic, Baptist, Methodist and Lutheran. "In the national picture, the much publicized cults and new religions vanish into statistical insignificance," Kosmin says.

— *Desda Moss*

Using Visual Aids

1. *Pay attention to visual aids.* Pictures, charts, graphs, illustrations, and maps add important information to what you're reading.
2. *Examine titles, captions, or other explanations that appear with visual aids.* Accompanying words and sentences often point out the main features of the illustrations.
3. *Connect the illustrations with the sentences and paragraphs of the selection.* As you're reading, stop and ask yourself key questions. What does the illustration show? Why has it been included? What does it show that the words do not?
4. *Put visual information in your own words.* Compose sentences in your mind that explain the illustrations provided.

4

Reading for the Main Idea

4a   Key Ideas in Sentences

Although a sentence may give a great deal of information, it usually offers one key idea. The key idea of a sentence usually tells

- who a person or what an object is
- what a person or an object is doing

| WHO IS DOING SOMETHING | WHAT THE PERSON (OR OBJECT) IS DOING |

A tall girl in a white dress rushed away into the trees

just beyond the gate to Stevens Park.

This sentence tells about a girl. We know that the girl rushed away. All the information about her appearance, about where she ran, and about the name of the park adds details. These are helpful in completing the scene for the reader, and very often we need to rely on details to make the main text clearer. But the key idea, the main thought, in the sentence is simply *a girl rushed away.*

How to Find Key Ideas in Sentences

- Ask *whom* or *what* the sentence is about.
- Ask what the person or object is doing or what is happening to that person or object.
- Learn to separate minor details from the main idea. Many words in sentences describe things about the subject of the sentence and merely add details around it. If you ask *when, what kind, where,* or *why,* you will find details. This makes it easier to separate the key idea.

(*why*)   (*what kind*)
Because of new laws, most foreign automobiles in the

   (*where*)   (*when*)   (*how*)
United States now offer safety features at no extra charge.

Who or what is the sentence about? *automobiles*
What do the automobiles do? *offer safety features*
The key idea is *automobiles offer safety features.*

Of course, you cannot always decide easily which details are simply descriptive and which contribute markedly to the key idea. In stating a key idea, you may have to shift around words in the sentence and you may have to summarize parts of the sentence. It's always a good idea to try to put some of the writer's words into your own words.

The starting point for determining the key idea in a sentence, however, is finding who or what the sentence is about and what the person or object is doing.

The following word chart shows further examples of key ideas in sentences from textbooks.

Key Ideas in Textbooks

Biology

Even the simplest organisms consist of many parts and each of these must do the right thing at the right time for an appropriate action to be carried out.

— *John W. Kimball*

Key Idea

Each part of an organism must work properly so that the organism can carry out actions.

Marketing

By bridging the market separations, marketing creates utility or value for the parties in the exchange.

— *Thomas Kinnear and Kenneth Bernhardt*

Key Idea

Marketing creates value.

Chemistry

Because of its cheapness and ready availability, oxygen is one of the most widely used industrial oxidizing agents.

— *Mitchell J. Sienko and Robert A. Plane*

Key Idea

Oxygen is widely used in industry.

Communication

Encoding is the act of producing messages—such as speaking, writing or gesturing.

— *Joseph A. Devito*

Key Idea

Encoding is making messages.

Psychology

Social role theories stress social expectations and the relationship between hypnotist and subject; according to these theories, the subject is doing what he or she believes is appropriate in the social situation.

— *James D. Laird and Nicholas S. Thompson*

Key Idea

Social role theories say subjects of hypnotism act as they think appropriate to the situation.

Economics

A market makes possible the exchange of goods and services between buyers and sellers, and that exchange determines the price of goods and services.

Key Idea

A market makes possible exchanges between buyers and sellers.

Buyers and sellers communicate with each other about the quality and quantity, what the buyers are willing and able to pay, and what the sellers must receive.

— *William Boyes and Michael Melvin*

Buyers and sellers communicate.

Law	*Key Idea*
William Blackstone, an English judge and author of *Commentaries on the Laws of England* (1765–1769), defined a crime as a wrong committed against the public, a definition that is still widely recognized as appropriate.	**A crime is a wrong against the public.**
Defining a wrong against the public is a responsibility of the government.	**The government defines public wrongs.**
In a democracy, this necessarily involves a balancing of interests: society needs to protect itself and its citizens from harm, but society must also protect the rights of individuals to be free from undue government interference.	**A democracy balances protection and the rights of its citizens.**

— *Harold Grilliot and Frank Schubert*

4b Topics and Main Ideas in Paragraphs

A *paragraph* is a group of sentences about some related subject or topic. Each sentence states some idea about the *topic,* and all those ideas add up to an overall *main idea* of the paragraph.

A main idea is not simply a topic. A topic is just the general subject that a paragraph deals with. A main idea, on the other hand, is the statement the paragraph makes about the topic. You often can state a topic in a single word; but to state a main idea clearly, you usually need a full sentence.

Who has not felt a little thrill when about to hop onto an escalator? You step onto an already moving platform that unfolds itself into a staircase to sweep you upward above your plainly visible surroundings. The ride might almost have been created as an amusement-park attraction, yet it is so safe and mild it plays an unremarked role in our daily lives. The design seems fixed and basic, but it evolved in imperfect forms over three decades before a melding of ideas in the 1920s produced the escalator as we know and ride today.

— *William Worthington*

The topic of the above paragraph is, simply, "the escalator"; but to answer the question "What about the escalator?" you would have to state the main idea more fully: "Although an escalator ride may be thrilling, escalators are considered a safe, unremarkable part of our daily lives."

Substances found in the environment that are essential to the body's function are *minerals.* Minerals are used to regulate a wide range of body processes, from bone formation to blood clotting. They are also important to the body's structure. Except for iron, the body does not tend to store minerals. Iron tends to be conserved by the body, except when there is blood loss. Most minerals are quickly used or lost in waste products. This means you must eat mineral-rich foods regularly to replenish your supply. Your body uses larger amounts of calcium, phosphorous, and magnesium than of iodine, iron, and zinc.

— *Bud Getchell, Rusty Pippin, and Jill Varnes*

In the same way, the topic of the paragraph at the bottom of page 60 is "the body's use of minerals." To express the main idea, however, requires a full sentence: "Minerals are essential to the body's function." This sentence makes a statement about the topic. The statement is a general idea that covers all the specific ideas in the paragraph.

In order to understand the meaning of a paragraph, readers must identify,

- the **topic of the paragraph**
- the **main idea being presented about that topic.**

The topic may be stated in only a word or two, naming a thing, person, or event discussed throughout the paragraph. The main idea, however, is a more complete statement that ties all the ideas and information in the paragraph together. Writers state the main idea of a paragraph directly in a sentence, or they may imply it in the overall message of all the sentences. With a directly stated main idea, you need locate only the main idea sentence. With an implied main idea, you must figure out the topic of the paragraph and the idea being stated about that topic.

 APPLICATIONS: Your Courses

As you read for your courses, be sure that you understand the relation between the topic and the main idea.

4b(1) *Stated Main Ideas*

Often one sentence in the paragraph tells the reader exactly what the rest of the paragraph deals with. Therefore, that sentence gives the main idea. This *main idea sentence* (it is often called a *topic sentence* or *topic statement*) may appear in one of several places.

Main Idea in the Beginning

MAIN IDEA AT
BEGINNING

As the sun went down, the scene from the bridge was beautiful. It has been a perfect day. Up and down on either side of New York the bright blue water lay gently rippling, while to the south it merged into the great bay and disappeared toward the sea. The vast cities spread away on both sides. Beyond rolled the hilly country until it was lost in the mists of the sky. All up and down the harbor the shipping, piers, and buildings were still gaily decorated. On the housetops of both Brooklyn and New York were multitudes of people.

— David McCullough

The main idea of this passage is *the scene from the bridge was beautiful.* All the sentences in the paragraph illustrate that idea by providing many details.

Main Idea in the Middle

There are 74.5 million television sets in the United States, at least one set for 98 percent of all American homes. Forty-eight percent of all U.S. homes have more than one set, and some families even have a set for every person in the house. *Yet despite the fact that the number of sets in the United States has virtually reached a saturation point, the amount of time spent watching television has declined steadily since 1976.* Explanations vary from the increasingly poor quality of network shows to the rising popularity of home video equipment, but the fact remains that we are owning more sets but enjoying them less.

MAIN IDEA IN MIDDLE

The main idea of this paragraph is *despite the fact that the number of television sets in the United States has virtually reached a saturation point, the amount of time spent watching television has declined steadily since 1976.*

Main Idea at the End

Although the buildings are tall, none of them blots out the sky. People rush about as in New York, but someone always stops to answer a question about directions. A person will listen when he or she is asked a question. Often a sudden smile will flash from the crowds of strangers pushing down State Street. It is a smile of welcome and of happiness at the same time. And the traffic: it is tough, noisy, active; but a person never feels as if he takes his life in his hands when he crosses the street. Of course, there is always the presence of the lake, the vast, shimmering lake that shines like an ocean of silver. Something about that lake each time it spreads out around a turn on Lakeshore Drive says, "Hello. It's good to see you again." *Chicago is a fine, friendly city.*

MAIN IDEA AT THE END

The main idea in the paragraph is *Chicago is a fine, friendly city.* All the other sentences in the paragraph support that idea with details. By stating the main idea at the end, the author summarizes the point of the paragraph.

Main Idea in More than One Sentence

MAIN IDEA IN TWO SENTENCES

Dogs make warm, friendly pets. However, they can also be very troublesome. No one will deny the feelings of friendship when after a master's long day's work, a wet pink tongue of greeting licks his hand at the door. And watching television or reading a book, a man or woman can reach down over the side of the couch and feel a warm furry patch of life, hear the quiet contented breathing of a good friend. However, try to plan a trip without your faithful pet and your life is very difficult. Where will you leave him? Who will feed him? Further, leaving a cozy house in the midst of winter and facing a howling frozen wind so the dog may take his walk is no pleasure at all. I often wonder why people put up with such demands upon their time and energy.

The main idea in this paragraph appears in two sentences. Although the first sentence of the selection says that dogs are warm, friendly pets, only part of the paragraph gives details to support the idea. Other details in the paragraph show that dogs are troublesome. An accurate statement of the main idea would have to include the information in both of the first two sentences: *Dogs make friendly pets, but they can also be troublesome.*

4(b)2 *Implied Main Ideas*

Sometimes paragraphs do not state exactly what the topic is. Instead, you must decide on the main idea yourself. In order to do that, you must add up all the details the writer gives and then state the main idea in your own words.

When the writer has not stated a main idea exactly, but instead *suggests* the idea to you through information in the paragraph, the idea is *implied*. An *implied main idea* is one that is suggested.

A lot of people assume it's nutritionally better to buy dark breads. We tend to believe that white bread has the nutrients processed out, while dark bread still has them inside. Not necessarily true. Dark bread is sometimes simply white bread, dyed dark. There's no definite data on what bread may be better for you, but consider this: Consumers Union bought thirty-three brands of bread and fed them to laboratory rats. Then they weighed and measured to see how much each rat grew or did not grow. The study found it made no difference whether the rats ate dark or white bread. It also made no difference whether the bread was "enriched." The bread companies that I called said the test was ridiculous, since no one eats only bread. Nutritionists I called said if you want a more nutritious bread, buy whole wheat. Whole wheat has more nutrients left in. The word "wheat" alone, or "health food" bread doesn't mean anything.

— John Stossel

What is the topic of this paragraph? Clearly, the writer is talking about the nutritional value of breads. Knowing the topic helps you figure out the main idea. But in this paragraph, the writer never directly tells you the main idea of the paragraph: *White bread is probably just as nutritious as most dark breads, except for whole wheat.* You have to figure it out from the various details the writer gives you.

Finding Implied Main Ideas

- Look at all the ideas and details in the paragraph.
- Ask if the ideas and details all relate to a single person or object. What is that topic? Then check all the sentences of the paragraph (not just the first few) to make sure that they really are all about your suggested topic. If not, try to find a topic that fits all the sentences. As you have seen, all the sentences in the example on pages 64–65 discuss the nutritional value of different breads.

- Ask what point all these ideas and details are making about that topic. Then write a complete sentence that (1) names the person or thing and (2) tells what that person or thing is doing. Again check all the sentences of the paragraph to make sure that they fit your main idea sentence. If they do not, you must make your point broader so that it covers everything in the paragraph. The sentence "Whole wheat bread is nutritious" does not cover the whole main idea in the paragraph.

- Be sure that your implied main idea sentence is not too general. Can you make the topic more specific, or can you say something more specific about the topic and still be describing all the sentences in the paragraph? If you can, you should make your sentence more specific. If your sentence covers all the sentences in the paragraph and cannot be made any more specific, then it is correct. The topic sentence "All breads have some nutrition" would be too general for the example. Only the sentence given— *White bread is probably just as nutritious as most dark breads, except for whole wheat*—is neither too narrow nor too general.

Read this paragraph for another implied main idea.

Sociologists reserve the term *small group* to refer to a group small enough for all members to interact simultaneously, that is, to talk with each other or at least be acquainted with each other. Small groups such as work groups and families are the intermediate link between the individual and the larger society. This intermediate position defines their importance in terms of attitudes, values, and behaviors. For this reason, sociologists are interested in what happens when people get together in small groups, whether it is to share gossip, reach a decision, or even play card games.

— *Richard T. Schaefer*

You know that the topic here is *small groups*. But what point is the writer making about small groups? What is the main idea of the paragraph? The writer implies it; he doesn't state it directly. Using the pointers explained in the box on pages 65–66, you should be able to state the main idea in your own words. You might say something like this: *Sociologists study small groups because they are important in understanding how people relate to one another.*

Note the main ideas as you read these selections from several different college disciplines.

Marketing

Eastman Kodak Co., one of the world's leading photographic companies, makes innovation a part of its everyday company strategy. Recently, Kodak introduced a line of single-use, or disposable, cameras. These cameras are very simple to operate: all one needs to do is aim and push a button. There are no adjustments for light level, exposure time, or focusing. After shooting all the exposures, the customer turns in the entire camera to the film processor. Depending on the model, these cameras retail from $8.35 for the Fling, to around $14 for the more specialized models. One model is a modified wide-angle camera; another can take pictures up to twelve feet underwater. They all use 35mm color film. Very inexpensive to produce, these cameras are basically just a roll of film in an encasement of plastic that has an elementary lens on the front and a minimum of internal parts. Kodak executives hope that the disposable cameras (Kodak prefers the name "single-use" cameras) become highly profitable.

— *William Pride and O. C. Ferrell*

Main Idea: The single-use camera is an example of Kodak's innovative strategy.

History

The dethronement of Louis XVI, the establishment of a republic in September 1792, and the king's execution in January 1793 were all signs of growing radicalism. As the new Republic tottered under the twin blows of internal insurrection and foreign invasion, the revolutionary leadership grew more extreme. In June 1793 the Jacobins took power. Tightly organized, disciplined, and fiercely devoted to the Republic, the Jacobins mobilized the nation's material and human resources to defend it against the invading foreign armies. To deal with counterrevolutionaries, the Jacobins unleashed the Reign of Terror, which took the lives of some 20,000 to 40,000 people, many of them innocent of any crime against the state. Although the Jacobins succeeded in saving the Revolution, their extreme measures aroused opposition. In the last part of 1794, power again passed into the hands of the moderate bourgeoisie who wanted no part of Jacobin radicalism.

— *Marvin Perry*

Main Idea: The events and forces that gave the radical Jacobins power also caused them to destroy themselves.

Psychology

A second stubborn controversy concerns the existence of sex differences in the brain. Efforts to distinguish male from female brains have a long and not always glorious history in psychology. During the nineteenth century, "findings" on male-female brain differences often flip-flopped in a most suspicious manner (Shields, 1975). At first, scientists doing dissection studies reported that women's frontal lobes were smaller than men's, and that their parietal lobes were larger. This presumably explained women's intellectual shortcomings. Then, around the turn of the century, people began (mistakenly) to attribute intellect to the parietal lobes rather than the frontal lobes. Suddenly there were reports that women had *smaller* parietal lobes and larger frontal lobes. You probably won't be surprised to learn that these researchers often knew the sex of the brains they were dissecting.

— *Carole Wade and Carol Tavris*

Main Idea: Differences between men and women in brain anatomy that were used to explain differences in intelligence often had no basis in objective science.

Ecology

 Certain terms are used in ecology to provide a consistent description of conditions and events. A *population* refers to all of the members of a given species that live in a particular location. For example, a beech-maple forest will contain a population of maple trees, a population of beech trees, a population of deer, and populations of other species of plants and animals. All of the plant and animal populations living and interacting in a given environment are known as a *community*. The living community and the nonliving environment work together in a cooperative ecological system known as an *ecosystem*. An ecosystem has no size requirement or set boundaries. A forest, a pond and a field are examples of ecosystems. So is an unused city lot, a small aquarium, the lawn in front of a residential dwelling, or a crack in a sidewalk. All of these examples reflect areas where interaction is taking place between living organisms and the nonliving environment.

— *Gabrielle I. Edwards*

Main Idea: Ecologists use terms like *ecosystem, population,* and *community* to describe conditions and events in a consistent way.

Economics

 The purpose of markets is to facilitate the exchange of goods and services between buyers and sellers. In some cases money changes hands; in others only goods and services are exchanged. The exchange of goods and services directly, without money, is called **barter.** Barter occurs when a plumber fixes a leaky pipe for a lawyer in exchange for the lawyer's work on a will; when a Chinese citizen provides fresh vegetables to an American visitor in exchange for a pack of American cigarettes; and when children trade baseball cards. Most markets involve money because goods and services can be exchanged more easily with money than without it. When IBM purchases microchips from Yakamoto of Japan, IBM and Yakamoto do not engage in barter. One firm may not have what the other wants. Barter requires a **double coincidence of wants:** IBM must have what Yakamoto wants, and Yakamoto must have what IBM wants. The **transaction costs** (the costs involved in making an exchange) of finding a double coincidence of wants for barter transactions are typically very high. Money reduces these transaction costs. To obtain the microchips, all IBM has to do is provide dollars to Yakamoto. Yakamoto accepts the money because it can spend the money to obtain the goods that it wants.

— *William Boyes and Michael Melvin*

Main Idea: Markets allow the exchange of goods and services through either money or barter.

APPLICATIONS: Your Courses

As you examine texts for your courses, be sure that you can determine the main idea of what you read. Identify three different passages in a textbook you are using. For each, write the main idea in your own words.

5

Reading for Information

The main idea of a selection does not give you all the information you need. Facts and details develop the main ideas of the paragraphs. These facts and details may paint a more complete picture, give examples to help you understand the ideas better, prove a point, or show how the idea relates to other ideas. To make the best use of these facts and details, you have to be able to

■ find important facts and remember them.
■ separate major facts and details from minor facts and details.

5a Fact Finding

To find and remember important facts, you must be an active, aware reader. (See **1**.) Study the following list of tips; they will help you locate facts.

How to Locate Facts

- **Have a definite purpose for reading.** Are you reading a page of your biology book to find out how the eye works? Are you reading a chapter of

71

a political science text to learn the meaning of *democracy*? Are you reading the newspaper out of general interest or for a specific research project?

- **Learn to read for the main idea.** If you recognize the main idea easily, the facts to support that idea will stand out.
- **Know that not all facts and details are equal in importance.** Look only for the facts that relate to the main idea.
- **Look for information in groups or units.** Facts often appear together in bunches.
- **Look for the way the paragraph is put together.** How is the information arranged? Has the writer organized the material in terms of a pattern that is easy to see?
- **Learn to keep an author's *opinions* apart from the *facts* offered in the writing.**
- **Question yourself as you read.** Stop to think and to let facts sink in before you rush on to other information. Ask yourself, "What does that mean?" or "What does that information tell me?" or "Why is this information here?"
- **Use the five Ws when you read in order to ask yourself specific questions about the facts.**

    1. Ask yourself "Who?" Then look for the name of someone or something.
    2. Ask yourself "When?" Then look for a date (a day, a month, a year) or a time of day or year.
    3. Ask yourself "Where?" Then look for words that show a location or name a place.
    4. Ask yourself "What?" or "What happened?" Then look for some action.
    5. Ask yourself "Why?" Then look for an explanation of some act or event.

- **Think about the kinds of questions someone might ask you about the information you have read.** Go back after you have finished to reread quickly and review any facts you have learned. Try to summarize the important facts in your mind.

Look at the following selection about an unusual court case in the Philippines to see how the information is organized. The comments in the margin illustrate fact-finding.

20th-Century Lawsuit Asserts Stone-Age Identity

WHO?
WHEN?
WHAT HAPPENED?

Members of a primitive tribe claiming a jungle cave for its home took a giant step into the 20th century this week by filing a lawsuit against two anthropologists who say they are a hoax.   1

MORE INFORMATION
ON THE PEOPLE IN
THE STORY

"We are the forest," the tribeswoman Dul said gravely before affixing her thumbprint to the complaint. "We are the Tasaday."   2

"We are as real as the forest and the flowers and the trees and the stream," she said through an interpreter. "We are as strong as the stone of the cave of Tasaday."   3

WHERE ARE THEY
FROM?

The suit was filed Monday by four members of the group known as the Tasaday, who were first described in 1971 as a Stone Age tribe of forest gatherers who dressed in orchid leaves and bark and had no word for war, enemy or ocean.   4

Visits by Journalists

MORE INFORMATION
ON THE CONFLICT
THAT LED TO THE
COURT CASE

Since 1986 they have been in the news 5
again after visits by several journalists
who found them to possess bits of clothing, knives and trinkets and proclaimed
them to be a fraud perpetrated by
Ferdinand E. Marcos when he was
President.

WHO ARE THE
OPPONENTS IN THE
CONFLICT?

The group's complaint names the two 6
anthropologists who are among their
most insistent debunkers, Jerome Bailen
and Zeus Salazar of the University of the
Philippines, and asks that the Tasaday be
left in peace in the forest preserve set aside
by Mr. Marcos on Mindanao Island.

WHO?
WHAT IS THE
CONFLICT ABOUT?

The four tribespeople were joined in 7
their complaint by their protector, Manuel
Elizalde Jr., the man accused of concocting
the fraud in his role as Mr. Marcos's
Minister for Tribal Minorities.

Mr. Bailen has called the Tasaday "the 8
most elaborate hoax perpetrated on the
anthropological world" since the
Piltdown man, human skeletal remains
discovered in England in 1908, falsely

WHAT DOES ONE
SIDE BELIEVE?

attributed to the Lower Pleistocene epoch
and then proved a hoax in 1950.

Persuaded to Wear Leaves

He and Mr. Salazar say Mr. Elizalde, for 9
his own reasons, persuaded members of
another more advanced tribal group to
wear leaves, make stone implements and
pose as cave-dwellers.

WHAT DOES THE
OTHER SIDE BELIEVE?

The legal complaint insists that the 10
Tasaday are "a separate ethnic community" with their own language and forest
home who until this generation had

believed that they were the only people in the world.

It cites a still-unreleased report by a committee of the Philippine Congress that reverses that body's position and declares the group to be genuine. According to the report, those who cry fraud have failed to prove their case.   11

— *Seth Mydans*

For best reading results, you should have established a purpose in reading. Use the words *unusual court case in the Philippines* in the instructions to help yourself read for special information. Did you remember to ask yourself these questions as you read: What is the main idea? How is the information arranged? Which facts are most important? What questions might someone ask about this selection?

APPLICATIONS: Your Courses

Much of your course reading will require that you identify facts. Choose a textbook page for one of your courses and, applying the steps indicated in this section, identify important facts.

5b   Major Details, Minor Details

It's obvious that not all facts in a paragraph have the same importance. In the selection on pages 73–75, for example, the names of two anthropologists and the report of the Philippine Congress are among the less important details. Because you do not need these details to understand the selection, the information they give is minor. Minor details help round out a paragraph and often hold our attention to make the material we are reading more interesting. Still, we can ignore minor details if our goal is a quick understanding of what we've read. Details that give major information about the main idea, however, are very important.

How to Find Major Details

- State the main idea in your own words.
- Look only for information that supports the main idea.
- Read quickly over the words or sentences that give information that is not important to the main idea.
- Look for signal words like *most important*, *first*, *finally*, *the facts are*, and so on.
- Underline or highlight the major details when you locate them.

Here is how one student used underlining to separate the major details from the minor details in a passage she was reading to learn about *culture shock* for her course in sociology.

Anthropologists use the term "culture shock" to describe the impact of a totally new culture upon a newcomer. In an extreme instance such shock will be experienced by the Western explorer who is told halfway through dinner, that he is eating the nice old lady he had been chatting with the previous day—a shock with predictable physiological if not moral consequences. Most explorers no longer encounter cannibalism in their travels today. However, the first encounters with polygamy or with puberty rites or even with the way some

Main Idea:
Sociologists, like anthropologists, get shocked
by a culture, but the
sociologist looks at his
own culture instead of
foreign ones.

nations drive their automobiles can be quite a shock to an American visitor. <u>With the shock may go not only disapproval or disgust but a sense of excitement that things can *really* be that different</u> from what they are at home. To some extent, at least, this is the excitement of any first travel abroad. The experience of <u>soci-ological discovery</u> could be described as <u>"cul-ture shock" minus geographical displacement</u>. In other words, the sociologist travels at home—with shocking results. He is unlikely to find that he is eating a nice old lady for din-ner. But the discovery, for instance, that his own <u>church</u> has considerable <u>money invested in the missile industry</u> or that a few blocks from his home there are <u>people who engage in cultic orgies</u> may not be drastically different in emotional impact. Yet we would <u>not</u> want to imply that sociological discoveries are <u>always</u> or even usually <u>outrageous</u> to moral senti-ment. Not at all. What they have in common with exploration in distant lands, however, is the <u>sudden illumination of new and unsus-pected facets of human existence in society.</u>

— *Peter Berger*

Notice that by underlining, the student focuses only on details that help explain the main idea directly. Some of these details are the concept of cul-ture shock, the reaction to shocking events, and the kinds of shocking things that a sociologist can find in the United States.

Notice, too, those details the student passes over as not so important. Some unimportant details are the nice old lady being served for dinner, the decrease in cannibalism today, and the experience of the first trip abroad. These minor details make the main idea more vivid, but the main idea can be understood without them.

6

Recognizing Paragraph Patterns

Paragraphs present ideas and information in a connected web or pattern of meaning. Writers often help you discover this pattern of meaning by the way they arrange information or ideas. If you miss a paragraph's pattern and don't see how the details fit together, the paragraph will seem a jumble of confused ideas or facts to you. Once you are familiar with possible paragraph patterns, you will be able to spot them when you read.

For example, when you are able to recognize that a story unfolds in time order, you will immediately know how to put the details together in your mind. You will also know that each new sentence will answer the question "What happens next?" When you recognize a comparison-contrast pattern, you will know that the writer is presenting two sets of information—details for each of the two items being compared—and you can carefully match up every detail with its proper subject.

Writers often shift, overlap, and combine patterns. Sometimes they invent new ones. A paragraph that begins by following place order to set a scene may shift to time order to let the writer tell a story. When an order of importance emerges, the writer is conveying opinions about the material.

6a   Ordering of Ideas

6a(1)   *Time Order (Chronology)*

Some paragraphs present ideas in time order. Keep in mind the *sequence:* One idea follows another and relates to an event or idea that comes before. Writers often use this order to tell a story or to explain how to do or make something.

A small, hand-propelled German submarine, the *Brandtaucher,* sank in 1851 in sixty feet of water, with her captain, Wilhelm Bauer, and two crew members aboard. Her hull immediately began to collapse under the pressure of the sea. Captain Bauer, who had built the tiny craft, knew that if he could keep his two companions from panicking while allowing the water to rise steadily inside her, the interior and exterior pressure would equalize and they would be able to open the hatch and get out. They did. As Bauer wrote later, "We came to the surface like bubbles in a glass of champagne." The world made little note of this first escape from a sunken submarine.

— *Ann Jensen*

6a(2)   *Place Order*

Some paragraph details follow a direction that traces movement from one part of a scene to another—from left to right, from near to far, from east to west, or in some other clear place order.

As I look around this room in this third-rate boarding house, my eyes are greeted first by the entrance to its gloomy interior. The door is painted a dirty cream color. There is a crack in one panel. The ceiling is the same dingy color with pieces of adhesive tape holding some of the plaster in place. The walls are streaked and cracked here and there. Also on the walls are pieces of Scotch tape that once held, I presume, some sexy girls, pictures of *Esquire Magazine* origin. Across the room runs a line; upon it hang a shirt, a grimy towel, and washed stump socks belonging to my roommate, Jack Nager. By the door near the top sash juts a piece of wood on which is hung—it looks like an old spread. It is calico, dirty, and a sickly green color. Behind that is a space which serves as our closet; next to that is the radiator, painted the same ghastly color. The landlady must have got the paint for nothing. On top is Jack's black suitcase, his green soap dish, and a brightly colored box containing his hair tonic. Over by the cracked window are a poorly made table and chair. On top of the table, a pencil, shaving talcum, a glass, a nail file; one of my socks hangs over the side. Above the table is our window, the curtains of cheese cloth held back by a string. There is also a black, fairly whole paper shade to dim such little sunlight as might enter.

— John J. Regan

6a(3) *Order of Importance*

Some paragraph details are put together so that we know which ideas the writer thinks are more important. Generally, the least important idea comes first, with the other details presented in order of growing importance and the most important idea coming last.

There are several good reasons why the United States needs to involve private businesses in the space program. First, the federal government can't afford to invest in expensive projects and fight the deficit at the same time. Second, few people in government today have the vision to propose the next step in space exploration or the political prestige to make that vision a reality. Private corporations have both the resources and the motivation to explore space. New discoveries will aid business and give the world new sources of minerals and energy. With a little encouragement corporations could begin sending probes or even piloted missions to explore the solar system. Private business involvement would open the universe to the same forces that created new settlements and colonies on earth. The added advantage is that we could accomplish in decades what would otherwise take centuries at the rate NASA is advancing.

How to See the Order of Details in a Paragraph

- Certain words in paragraphs give you hints about how the ideas are arranged.
- For *time order* look for words that tell time, such as *when, then, first, second, next, last, after, before, later, finally.*
- For *place order* look for words that locate, such as *there, beside, near, above, below, next to, under, over, alongside, beneath, by, behind, on.*
- For *order of importance* look for words that help us judge importance, such as *first, next, last, most important, major, greatest, in the first place.*

6b   Listing of Details

Information in a paragraph sometimes appears just as a series of facts or details. In other words, the paragraph presents a listing of information. Notice how the following example tells about conditions in America during the Great Depression.

In 1935 the depression in America was five years old and deepening. America had over 19,000,000 people on relief, one in every six or seven of the population. As FERA administrator, Harry Hopkins had spent $323,890,560 on relief in the first ten months of 1934, almost a third more than in 1933. In 1935 Congress appropriated $4,880,000,000 for the Work Relief Bill. *Time* estimated uncomfortably that of the 19,000,000 on relief, 20 percent were unemployables, or "chronic dependents." Over the country the debate ran, "Most people out of work couldn't hold jobs if they had them." For the first time since 1911, marriages had fallen in 1932 below the one-million mark, though the population had risen from 93,000,000 in 1911 to 125,000,000 in 1932. In 1935, according to the President's inaugural statement of 1937, one-third of American families were "ill-fed, ill-clothed, and ill-housed." The mean income of 13,000,000 families was $471 annually, including income from gardens and part-time labor. For these families the average expenditure for food was $206 annually. The middle third of American families received a mean income of $1,076; the upper third received an average of $2,100.

— *Don M. Wolfe*

Understanding the Listing of Details

- Determine the main idea.
- Look for new facts or new ideas in each sentence.
- Connect the various facts to the main idea of the paragraph.
- Separate major details from minor.
- Look for dates or other sequence indicators (the words *first, second, third,* and so on) as possible cues for the listing of details.

6c Classification

In some paragraphs different details relating to a topic are arranged in categories, or groups. This paragraph pattern, called *classification*, identifies categories, shows how various examples in the same category are alike, and shows how the separate categories are different. Classification can also show how a large subject may be broken up into different parts. In reading paragraphs organized according to classification, notice what kinds of categories separate the specifics into groups.

The following paragraphs, for example, first classify the courts in the United States according to two categories, depending on whether the courts correspond to government level or to type of case. Then the classification continues, to explain the kinds of disputes the courts try to resolve.

There are several different kinds and levels of courts in the United States. Some correspond to the different branches of government. These include municipal (or city) courts, county courts, state courts, and federal courts, all the way up to the Supreme Court of the United States. Specialized courts deal with specific kinds of cases. There are divorce courts, for example, as well as traffic courts, small claims courts, and courts that do nothing but handle appeals from the decisions of other courts.

The basic function of all these courts can be stated very simply: It is to resolve disputes. But that simple statement masks an extremely complicated reality. Just as there are many kinds of courts, those courts are called upon to resolve many kinds of disputes. Some disputes are between private individuals, as when one person sues another for breaking a contract. Other disputes may be between a branch of government and a private person, as when a citizen is sued for underpayment of taxes, or when an individual sues the government for violation of his or her rights. Still other disputes may be between governments—the government of a state, for example, and the federal government—or even between different agencies of the same level of government.

Many disputes have to do with business matters, particularly with the interpretation of contracts. Some have to do with public questions, such as the application of the Constitution or of lesser laws. Another large category of disputes consists of criminal matters, cases in which the government of a particular state, or the federal government, accuses an individual of committing a crime.

— *Michael Kronenwetter*

Understanding Classification

- Determine the main idea.
- Identify the large group and the subgroups being highlighted.
- Look for words like *categories, groups, classify, classification, kinds, level,* and so on as possible cues to classification strategies.
- Distinguish the features that identify the members of each group.

6d Comparison and Contrast

Writers use comparison and contrast to relate one object to another by showing how they are alike and how they are different. In this example, the writer compares the usefulness of learning to lie for natural liars and for those without natural skill in lying.

While there could be a school for lie catchers, a school for liars would not make sense. <u>Natural liars don't need it, and the rest of us</u> *NATURAL LIARS* ———→ <u>don't have the talent to benefit from it.</u> Lying well is a special talent, not easily acquired. One must be a natural performer, winning and charming in manner. Such people are able, without thought, to manage their expressions, giving off just the impression they seek to con- *MOST PEOPLE* ———→ vey. They don't need much help. Most people need that help, but lacking a natural ability to perform, they will never be able to lie very well. Lying can't be improved by knowing what to do and what not to do. And I seriously doubt that practice will have much benefit. A self-conscious liar, who planned each move as he made it, would be like a skier who thought about each stride as he went down the slope.

— *Paul Ekman*

Another type of comparison and contrast allows the writer to state one point and discuss *both* objects in regard to that idea; then to state another point and discuss both objects in regard to *that* idea; and so on.

While there are many differences between high school and college, I'd have to say that the most important ones all involve freedom. Everyone has to attend high school, at least *ONE POINT* ———→ until tenth grade, so very often you find classes where the students aren't serious about learning. College is exactly the opposite. People are there voluntarily because they want to learn and improve themselves. As a result college students are much more serious and interested. Another major difference is that *A SECOND POINT* ———→ colleges don't enforce arbitrary rules. In high school you need a pass to be in the hallway during class, and you can't leave a classroom without permission. On the other hand, college

A THIRD POINT ———→ students can go where they please. No one asks them for passes and if they need to leave a class to make a phone call or go to the bathroom, they just leave. Finally, in high school classes are assigned and the same classes are held each day. However, in college, most classes meet only two or three days a week, and students have many options about which classes to take.

Understanding Comparison and Contrast

- Look for key words that help relate the two objects or ideas. These words point to like ideas:

similarly	in addition	in the same way
also	further	likewise

  These words point to ideas that differ:

but	on the other hand	still
although	in contrast	in spite of
however	yet	even so
nevertheless	conversely	nonetheless

- Look for a sentence or two that tells just what is being compared to what.
- As you read, keep in mind the two ideas that the writer is comparing or contrasting. Ask yourself: "What things are being compared? Why are they being compared? How are the things alike or different?"

6e   Cause and Effect

In this kind of paragraph, you learn either *why* something happened or what happened *as a result* of something. The writer may explain what *causes* a certain situation or what *results* from a situation.

Have you ever had the experience of putting money into a soda machine or a pay phone and instead of getting soda or a dial tone, you got nothing? Even though you know it's just a machine, how many of you find yourselves kicking a machine or giving it a frustrated shake? It may interest you to know that scientists have studied this behavior, which is called the *pain-attack mechanism*. Pigeons were trained to peck at a disk mounted on a wall and to expect the reward of some grain every time they did so. Scientists found that when they didn't reward the pigeon as it expected, the bird became very agitated, attacking the wall disk and even other pigeons in the same box. In similar experiments, monkeys, rats, and pigeons also reacted violently when they were given an electric shock for no reason. From these results, scientists decided that animals, and in a sense this includes us, will respond to a painful event by fighting back. The event can be physical pain, such as an electric shock, or emotional pain, such as expecting a reward and not getting it. But it also seems that getting yelled at or being fired, like losing a lover or losing money in a soda machine, will trigger anger or aggression in humans.

The following chart provides some key points for understanding cause and effect.

Understanding Cause and Effect

- If the writer tells why something happened, what happened because of something, or what might happen because of something, you can expect reasons to explain causes or effects.
- Look for word clues: *because, since, as a result, therefore, consequently, so.*
- Remember that many causes can contribute to a single effect and that many effects can stem from a single cause.

 APPLICATIONS: Your Courses

Select a page from a textbook you are using in one of your courses. Identify the various paragraph patterns you find on the page.

Unit
Two

Interpretation and Evaluation

7

Making Inferences

Inference is a process by which readers go beyond surface details and "read between the lines" to reach information logically. When you read, certainly, you develop ideas from the exact information you have

Schools do more than teach the "three Rs"—reading, 'riting, and 'rithmetic. They also attempt to control and regulate the behavior of students, reflecting the social values of the dominant society.

before you. Factual details in what you read provide the basis of your knowledge. But not every bit of information is easily apparent or clearly stated. Hints or suggestions may appear that you have to build on with your own knowledge and experience in order to understand something fully. Because information is not always stated in exact terms, readers supply their own information from details or ideas that are only suggested by the writer.

Look at page 90 for a visual presentation from a chapter on education in a sociology book. The subject of the photograph is children playing an exercise game outdoors.

Now look at the picture on page 90 again to answer these questions.

1. The figures in the picture are probably
   a. teenagers.
   b. sixth graders.
   c. first graders.

2. The picture shows a
   a. hot summer afternoon.
   b. day in early spring.
   c. cold winter morning.

3. The scene takes place
   a. on a city street.
   b. in a suburban mall or shopping center.
   c. in a playground or park.

None of the answers you chose is stated exactly by the description of the subject, or main idea, of the picture: *children playing an exercise game outdoors.*

To answer question 1, you looked at the size, actions, and clothing of the figures in the photograph.

The hints in the picture enabled you to reject the choices other than *c*. The figures could be neither teens nor sixth graders.

To answer question 2, you had to look expressly at what the children were wearing. You can tell that since their jackets are zipped to their necks, the children are dressed too warmly for a hot summer afternoon but probably not warmly enough for a cold winter morning. Besides, the children are not wearing gloves, almost a required piece of apparel for cold winters. You inferred that it is spring by the leaves on the bush in the background, as well as the lightweight clothing and outdoor play.

For question 3 you can eliminate *a* and *b* easily. Nothing in the photograph suggests that this is a scene on a city street or in a suburban mall or shopping center. Besides, the organized play of the children as well as the playground equipment in the background—a slide, perhaps—and the rough dirt-and-pebble ground all imply very strongly that this is a scene in a schoolyard or park.

Using inference, you went beyond the surface meaning of the picture to extract further information.

In reading words and sentences in a textbook, inference is an important skill because it helps us fill in information a writer only suggests. Now look at the written caption accompanying the photograph that you just examined. See if you can say why the writers included the picture in their chapter on education. Using inference about the sentences and the photograph together, look at the questions that follow and answer them.

1. We may infer from the caption that the main purpose of education is to teach
   a. basic skills.
   b. games.
   c. social values.

2. The writer chose a picture of children in line performing a group activity to show
   a. that education can be fun.
   b. basic skills education.
   c. how schools regulate and control students' behavior.
3. According to the writer, regarding these regulated and controlled games, the dominant society
   a. opposes them.
   b. praises them.
   c. links them to the three Rs.

To answer all these questions, you had to use inference regarding the caption and the photograph together.

In question 1, the writer is using the photograph of children at play to suggest an element in education beyond what people generally expect. The words about schools—"they *also* attempt to control and regulate the behavior of students"—support the idea that teaching social values is not usually considered the main purpose of education. True, it is important to teach social values to children; but social values are not seen as the primary educational goal. Answer *c* is not correct.

Even though we see the children at play, nothing in the photo or caption suggests that playing games is the main purpose of education either. Answer *b* is incorrect, too.

We have to infer here that transmission of knowledge is the key educational goal, named here in the caption as "the 'three Rs'—reading, 'riting, and 'rithmetic" and in the question as "basic skills." We add up this information to choose answer *a* as the only reasonable response.

For question 2, we can reject choice *b* right away. Nothing in the photograph links up to the idea of basic skills education. Further, although education may be fun, and the children in the photo may be enjoying themselves, we cannot infer that the writer chose the photo to make the point about learning and pleasure. Choice *a* is wrong, too. The main point of the caption is to state the schools' role in promoting society's values by controlling and regulating children's behavior. The boys and girls at play in the organized activity shown in the photo illustrate regulated behavior. Thus, we infer that choice *c* is correct.

For question 3, only *b* is correct. We know from the caption that regulated behavior reflects the dominant society's values, so we must reject choice *a*. The society does not oppose regulated games. In addition, although the caption mentions basic skills as an element in schools' teaching programs, the dominant society does not link the three Rs and organized games. Choice *c* is obviously wrong. If the dominant society reflects its social values in the regulated behavior of children, and organized games are examples of that regulated behavior, then we must infer that the society approves of controlled games for children. Answer *b* is the only acceptable answer here.

Using Inference

- Try to read beyond the words. Fill in details and information based on the writer's suggestions.
- Question yourself as you read. "Why is this person doing what she is doing?" you might ask as you read. "What can I infer from the scene?" Supply the answers on the basis of the writer's hints and your own experience.

- If a writer describes a person, try to understand the person from how she moves, what she says, what she looks like. You can infer things about character from the way a person behaves. Try to build a picture of the person in your mind; base your picture on the writer's description of action and appearance.
- If you find that you cannot easily answer a question about what you have read, remember to use inference skills. Return to the part of the reading where you expect the answer. Then see if the writer suggests something that you yourself have to supply in clearer terms.

APPLICATIONS: Your Courses

Read a selection from a textbook you are using. Make a list of the inferences you think you can draw from the selection.

8

Drawing Conclusions and Predicting Outcomes

Careful readers *interpret* what they read; that is, they try to explain and to understand ideas brought out by their reading. One way to build your skill at interpreting is to try to draw conclusions from what a writer tells you.

A reading selection gives you information about a topic. Good readers are able to use that information on their own in order to know what to expect next. Paragraphs or larger readings present information to support a topic, but they do not always state all the possible results of the events the writer discusses. In fact, if you must answer questions after you read, those questions often involve conclusions you must draw on your own.

But before you think of larger units like paragraphs or whole essays, it's useful to think about drawing conclusions from parts of individual sentences. Sometimes you can predict the outcome of a sentence—that is, you can make a reasonably accurate guess about how the sentence will end. You can use this skill to help yourself see how to draw conclusions and to predict outcomes in longer works.

Which word group from the choices given would you select to complete the following sentence?

If you keep reading books with small print in such dim light,

a. you'll never pass your exam.
b. you may not learn the meaning of important words.
c. you may strain your eyes.
d. you should play some music on the radio.

We can reasonably guess that *c* is the correct ending of the sentence. In fact, the only logical selection we can make from the choices given here is *c*.

We can tell from the word *if* that the writer is setting up conditions that will affect the outcome of the sentence. From the words in the sentence and from our own experiences, we know that small print and dim lighting can indeed lead to eyestrain. Although we cannot be absolutely certain that the writer had that point in mind, choice *c* would be a safe one.

Even though there may be some truth in the other choices, not one logically develops from the rest of the sentence. Choice *a* is not as good a choice as *c* because some people could pass an exam even though they read small print in poorly lit rooms. Similarly, you'd have to reject *b*; although you might have to squint, you could determine word meanings even if you read under poor conditions. Also, nothing in the first part of the sentence helps us predict that music would satisfy the meaning that the writer is aiming for. True, dim lighting and music sometimes go together, but in this example playing music is not a logical outcome, so choice *d* would be incorrect.

If you followed the preceding explanation, you have some idea about how to draw conclusions or to predict outcomes even in paragraphs and longer selections.

You have to put together facts and details logically in your own mind in order to draw the right conclusions.

You have to think ahead to events or ideas that might come from information the writer gives, information that forces you to *predict* how things come out.

Even though you might not know for sure, you have to use evidence you find in your reading to forecast what will happen.

Read this selection about the Gold Rush in the 1800s from a U.S. history textbook. Answer the questions after the selection to explore drawing conclusions and predicting outcomes.

The dream of finding precious metals beckoned people from near and far. Margaret Frink was one of thousands eager to "strike it rich." All across the Plains, she and her husband worried that "there would only be a few barrels of gold left for us when we got to California."

Prospectors such as the Frinks needed little experience and almost no capital. Placer mining—mining the deposits of a stream bed—could be done with a shovel, a washpan, and a good pair of eyes. (Hydraulic mining, a kind of placer mining in which miners blasted hillsides with thousands of gallons of water to wash gold-bearing soil and gravel into troughs, was more effective. It was also more expensive, however.)

Few of the early prospectors actually found much gold. Undaunted, they moved on to new sites. From California, many rushed to Colorado after the Pikes Peak gold strike of 1858–1859. Others headed for Nevada. Each prospector dreamed of the luck of Henry Comstock, whose claims in Nevada in 1859 ultimately brought forth hundreds of millions of dollars in gold and silver.

— *Thomas V. DiBacco, Lorna C. Mason, and Christian G. Appy*

1. We may conclude that Margaret Frink was originally from

a.   California.
b.   the Plains.
c.   the East.
2. If gold were discovered somewhere on the Plains, we may predict that the Frinks would
   a.   continue anyway toward their destination, California.
   b.   stop to try and strike it rich.
   c.   avoid prospecting because mining was too complicated.
3. We may predict that a prospector headed for a gold strike site would probably find
   a.   gold in a river bed.
   b.   only a few barrels of gold.
   c.   no gold.

If you chose *c* for question 1, how did you conclude that the Frinks were from the East? You knew, first, that they were heading toward California. You can guess that they didn't come from there originally. Choice *a* is not right. Second, the Frinks did travel over the American Plains. But the phrase in the text "all across the Plains" hints that the Frinks merely crossed the Plains on their way to somewhere else and did not live there. You should reject choice *b*. Although the text never mentions the East—the region of the United States stretching from the Atlantic Ocean—we have to conclude that the Frinks were traveling from somewhere east of both the Plains and California. Answer *c* is correct.

For question 2, we can reach a reasonable conclusion about the Frinks' behavior. We know that seeking gold propels their trip across the Plains. The whole selection is trying to show how "the dream of finding precious metals beckoned people from near and far." Thus, gold discovered anywhere in their path probably would stop the Frinks dead in their tracks. We must conclude that they would try to strike it rich where the gold was. Choice *b* is correct for question 2.

Though they are headed for California (the site of the earliest gold discoveries), no attraction other than wealth from gold draws them there. Thus, we have to reject choice *a*. And the text contradicts choice *c*. In truth, mining was so *un*complicated that all a prospector needed was "a shovel, a washpan, and a good pair of eyes."

In question 3, we know that the text says "Few of the early prospectors actually found much gold." By using inference and critical thinking skills to draw a valid conclusion, we also can predict a prospector's chances of actually finding gold. From those words we can conclude that a prospector headed for gold territory stood little chance of discovering the precious metal. Choice *c* is correct. True, some gold could be found in a river bed, but the odds were against the general prospector's finding gold at all. We must reject answer *a*. And gold was not found in barrels, although as Mrs. Frink used the term, a highly successful prospector, she imagined, might fill barrels with his new wealth, leaving little for her and her husband. Choice *b* is incorrect.

Now read the next selection, about foraging (how humans and other animals obtain food), from an anthropology text. The questions after the selection require active readers to draw conclusions and predict outcomes. Note the valid conclusions and predictions and the reasons for them.

[1]Despite their dependence on wild plants and animals, hunters and gatherers do not eat every edible species in their habitat. [2]They pass up many edible plants and animals even when they encounter them while searching for food. [3]Of some 262 species of animals known to the !Kung San, for example, only about 80 are eaten (Lee 1979:226). [4]This pickiness also occurs among ani-

mals that, like human hunter-gatherers, must *forage* (i.e., search) for their food.

[5]To account for this selective behavior, ecologists have developed a set of principles known as *optimal foraging theory* (Box 12.2). [6]This theory predicts that hunters or collectors will pursue or harvest only those species that maximize the rate of caloric return for the time spent foraging. [7]There will always be at least one species that will be taken on encounter, namely, the one with the highest rate of caloric return for each hour of "handling time"—time spent in pursuing, killing, collecting, carrying, preparing, and cooking the species after it is encountered. [8]The foragers will take a second, third, or fourth species when they encounter it only if by doing so it raises the rate of caloric return for their total effort (Charnov 1976; E. A. Smith 1983). [9]Of course, foragers do not actually measure how many calories they expend or obtain. [10]But through repeated trial and error, they achieve a rather precise knowledge of whether it is worth their while to take a particular species. [11](If lions and wolves can develop this selective behavior, so can humans!)

Box 12.2: An Intuitive Explanation of Optimal Foraging

[12]Imagine that you are in a forest in which some trees have a $1 bill and other trees have a $20 bill hanging from the topmost branches. [13]Should you climb every money tree you come across or should you climb only the $20 trees? [14]The answer depends on how many $20 money trees there are. [15]If there are a lot of them, it would be a mistake to climb $1 trees. [16]On the other hand, no matter how scarce $20 trees might be, if you happened to find one, you would always stop to climb it.

—*Marvin Harris*

Question: Who are the !Kung San?
Valid Conclusion: They are an African hunting-gathering people.
Evidence in Selection: *Sentences 1 and 3*—!Kung San serve as an example of "human hunter-gatherers" to establish a point about selective behavior for all animals.

Question: What has an owl learned who chooses to attack and eat a snake instead of a small bird?
Valid Conclusion: The snake provides a high rate of calories in return for "handling" time.
Evidence in Selection: *Sentences 2, 6, 7, and 8*—The selection makes no mention of owls, snakes, or small birds. Yet reading these sentences actively allows you to predict what animals have learned, if "optimal foraging" is a valid theory.

Question: In an imaginary forest with one $100 money tree for every fifty $5 money trees, what may we predict that most people will do?
Valid Conclusion: Most people will always climb the $100 tree, even if they sometimes climbed the $5 trees.
Evidence in Selection: *Sentences 12–16*—Note that the example in the selection compares $1 trees with $20 trees only.

Question: Why might an animal searching for food reject an edible plant or game?
Valid Conclusion: The species does not provide enough return for the energy needed to harvest or pursue it.
Evidence in Selection: *Sentences 1, 2, 4, 6, 7, and 10.*

How to Form Conclusions and Predict Outcomes

- Determine the main idea of the selection.
- Be sure you understand all the facts or details that the writer gives to support the idea.
- Check on difficult vocabulary. Did you use clues from the sentences (context clues) to figure out that *manna* had something to do with food? (Food supplied as if by a miracle—like the food that came to the Jews in the wilderness—is called *manna*.) (See **15a**, "Context clues for word meanings.")
- Look out for the logic of action. Did you follow the *sequence* (section **6a**)? Did you put events together in the right order of time or place to help yourself predict what would happen?
- Look at the way people are described. Can you tell from their personalities—from the way they think and feel—just how they might act?
- Ask yourself after you read: What will happen as a result of these actions or events?
- Build your conclusions on evidence you find in what you read, not exclusively on your own opinions, likes, and dislikes. Be careful not to read too much into a piece. Of course you need to allow your own experience to help you figure out how things may happen. But most of your conclusions must be based on what you read in the selection.

 APPLICATIONS: Your Courses

As you read a selection from a textbook for one of your courses, formulate conclusions about the selection and look ahead to possible outcomes.

9

Generalizing

Another way to help you interpret what you read is by developing skills in generalizing. When you *generalize*, you extend meanings beyond the specific ideas you read about. Generalizing allows you to apply information in a broader, less specific sense. You add up facts and details and draw from that particular information some general ideas or principles. One of the key aspects of critical reading for your courses is your ability to generalize from your textbooks and other assignments. Apply generalizing regularly to your course work.

Drawing conclusions and predicting outcomes (Chapter 8) are closely related to generalizing. *Generalizing* carries you a step beyond a conclusion that you can draw about a specific set of details. It's almost as if *you* develop a concept or a rule based on material you've read.

Read the following selection about the role of women in the ancient Greece *polis:* that is, the basic political and institutional unit, sometimes called the city-state. Then examine the questions and explanations that follow.

> The social condition of Athenian women has been the subject of much debate and little agreement. One of the difficulties is the fragmentary nature of the evidence. Women appear frequently in literature and art, often in idealized roles, but seldom in historical contexts of a wider and more realistic nature. This is due

in part to the fact that most Greek historians of the time recounted primarily the political, diplomatic, and military events of the day, events in which women seldom played a notable part. Yet that does not mean that women were totally invisible in the life of the polis. It indicates instead that ancient sources provide only a glimpse of how women affected the society in which they lived. Greek wives, for example, played an important economic and social role by their management of the household. Perhaps the best way to describe the position of the free woman in Greek society is to use the anthropologist's term *liminal,* which means in this case that although women lacked official power, they nonetheless played a vital role in shaping the society in which they lived. The same situation had existed in Hammurabi's Babylonia, and it would later recur in the Hellenistic period. The mere fact that Athenian and other Greek women did not sit in the assembly does not mean that they did not influence public affairs.

—*John P. McKay, Bennett D. Hill, and John Buckler*

1. We can conclude from this paragraph that women in Athens
   a. had a minor role in the larger society.
   b. served in official political positions.
   c. played a key role in society.
2. For societies in general, one is able to contribute to public affairs
   a. only through elective office.
   b. without having any formal authority.
   c. through idealized roles in literature and art.
3. In general, people excluded from historical records
   a. probably made very little contribution to their society.
   b. did not interest the historians or serve their goals.
   c. believed in ideas the historians opposed.

In question 1, the only valid conclusion to draw from this paragraph is that women played a key role in ancient Greek society, even though they did not have any official power. The paragraph disputes the "minor role" idea. Choice *a* is incorrect on the basis of points the authors make. Also, the selection insists that women had an important place in Greek life even though they had no official political positions. Choice *b* is incorrect. The only valid conclusion to draw from this paragraph is that women played a key role in Athenian society. Only choice *c* is a fair conclusion to draw for question 1.

In question 2, we must go beyond the conclusion we have drawn from the paragraph. From the historians who wrote the paragraph, we know that women had an important role in ancient Athens but that they had no official political status. The question asks us to consider women's places in other societies. Certainly we cannot say that only an elective office can provide someone with a voice in government. In regard to Greece, the paragraph contradicts that point. We must reject choice *a*.

And although written Greek records did not often show women in ideal roles, such roles had no direct link to public affairs. We cannot generalize to other societies that an idealized role for someone in literature or art means influence in public affairs. We must reject choice *c*.

Only choice *b* is correct. From the fact that women in Athens made important contributions without holding political positions, we can generalize to other societies. Even in our current world, people can contribute to the society's life without any formal authority. (Note that this generalization is valid for men, too.)

Question 3 asks you to make another generalization. Why do some people or issues simply not make their way into the history books? The selection says that Greek women played a major role in society even though historians did not write about them. We must assume that contributing to society is not necessarily a guarantee of being included in historical records. Choice *a* is incorrect.

Similarly, we have no evidence from the selection that disagreeing with historians automatically excludes a person from appearing in a historical record. Good historians will not allow personal likes and dislikes to determine what to write about. Historians may disagree with, even hate, some of the people they study. And they may say so in their descriptions. But a historian will not omit disagreeable characters or incidents on the basis of personal prejudice. We must reject choice *c*.

The selection states that events like wars and politics attracted the attention of Greek historians. Women played little part in those events, although they made other important, non-recorded contributions. We can generalize from this point that if a historian had no interest in a particular group of people, it might not find its way into the record. Thus, choice *b* is the only logical answer for question 3. In general, people excluded from historical records did not interest the historians or serve their goals. That is a fair generalization from this selection.

How to Generalize
- Make sure that you understand the main idea and key details from the reading.
- Make sure that you can draw conclusions or predict outcomes on the basis of information you have read.

- Think about how you might apply the writer's ideas in different situations.
- Don't go *too* far beyond the information the writer gives when you try to generalize. Otherwise, you face the problem of making statements that are too broad in scope.
- As you state a generalization, be particularly careful of words that do not allow exceptions. Words like *always, never, must, certainly, absolutely,* and *definitely* can rule out possibilities for any challenge to the general statement.
- Be aware that textbook writers will make generalizations as they analyze facts and events. A writer looking at an important issue often will generalize from the material at hand to a broader concept. Frequently, the generalization appears at the beginning of a paragraph or a selection, with supporting facts or details following to explain why the writer made the generalization. A main-idea statement is often a generalization.

Read the following selection about the development of sexual identity. Then examine the differences between valid and invalid generalizations that follow.

     ## Marriage and the Family

Exploration of bodies, "playing doctor," and other forms of sex play are quite common in childhood, but they seem to have more to do with curiosity about oneself and the parts adults regard as taboo than they do with satisfying a primordial urge. A good deal of behavior concerning sex roles is learned during childhood. But sexual experience as such begins at adolescence with the biological events of puberty. The timing of puberty varies, but girls generally undergo these changes between the ages of 12 and 14, and boys go through puberty about two years later. The complex changes of puberty begin in the brain with the signal to release certain hormones. Over a period of about two years, the reproductive organs mature, and adolescents develop sex characteristics, which give them the physical attributes of men or women. Although the physical events and sexual experiences of adolescence are quite different for male and female, the sense of oneself as a sexual being—a *sexual identity*—is part of the overall sense of individual identity that develops during the teenage years. The experience of socializing with the opposite sex and feeling desirable or undesirable, the events that surround sexual arousal, and the combination of guilt, anxiety, and satisfaction that accompanies such feelings—these are some of the elements that shape this new sense of sexual identity.

—*Diane I. Levande, Joanne B. Koch, and Lewis Z. Koch*

Valid Generalizations

- A young child who engages in sex play is merely exploring.
- A girl who undergoes puberty at the age of fifteen is not typical but not abnormal.
- Guilt and anxiety are normal consequences of early sexual arousal.
- Boys and girls alike form sexual identities in their teens.
- Sexuality involves both physical and emotional changes.

Invalid Generalizations

- Girls are more dependable than boys.
- Only girls develop adequate sexual identities.
- Adolescent boys and girls generally have similar sexual experiences.
- People develop a sense of sex roles with the onset of puberty.
- Children engaging in sex play are following a normal biological urge to satisfy sexual feelings.

APPLICATIONS: Your Courses

Read a selection in one of your textbooks. Then list three valid generalizations you can make.

10

Evaluating Ideas

Effective reading is more than just understanding text—you must be able to read *critically*, which means that you have to *evaluate* ideas once you understand them. When you evaluate a writer's ideas, you are judging the worth of what you read.

Evaluating What You Read: Key Questions to Ask Yourself

- Does the author carefully separate objective fact from opinion?
- Does the passage present the facts completely, specifically, and accurately?
- Does the author seem reliable? Can you see what strengths or experiences make the author qualified to write about a topic?
- Does the author make any claims that seem outrageous or insupportable?
- Does the intent or point of view of the author seem clear?
- Does the author take into account other points of view on the topic?
- Does the author try to appeal more to your emotions than to your reason and common sense?
- Does it seem that the author is slanting information in such a way as to prejudice your ideas? Is the author using propaganda?

10a Fact and Opinion

Look at the following two statements about the Christian teacher Saint Augustine, which come from *A History of Western Society* by John P. McKay, Bennett D. Hill, and John Butler.

1. Saint Augustine was born into an urban family in what is now Algeria in North Africa.
2. The finest representative of the blending of classical and Christian ideas, and indeed one of the most brilliant thinkers in the history of the Western world, was Saint Augustine of Hippo. (354–430)

Sentence 1 is a clear statement of fact. We have evidence that Saint Augustine was born in North Africa and that his family lived in the city. If we checked other sources—an encyclopedia or a biography—we would see that the statement is true.

In sentence 2, we cannot verify with factual checks all the information offered. The use of Augustine's full name and the dates of his birth and death create a sense of fact, providing data we can check, but in using words like "finest representative" and "one of the most brilliant thinkers," the writers are making a judgment about Saint Augustine. Because they are scholars of Western history—McKay, Hill, and Butler are college professors at the University of Illinois at Urbana-Champaign—we accept their statement easily. The writers' education and background tell us to rely on their assessment. We therefore accept it as valid.

In truth, many students of history would agree that Saint Augustine was a brilliant thinker who had a strong effect on religion by mixing Classical (Greek and Roman) and Christian ideas. Others might say, however, that Saint Paul or Saint Benedict, for example, were more influential Christian leaders. Still others might argue that Erasmus or John Skelton as thinkers represented a more forceful blend of Christian and Classical thought. None of these statements is incorrect. Yet each is an opinion.

Again, a strong opinion does not make a statement false or wrong. Nevertheless, an opinion is not a fact, and to judge a writer's work you have to be able to tell fact from opinion. Often writers will mix the two, some words representing facts and some, opinions. Think about the following sentences from an educational psychology textbook.

> You have probably heard and may even have used the term *hyperactivity*. The notion is a modern one: there were no children considered hyperactive 30–40 years ago. Today, if anything, the term is applied too often and too widely.
>
> — *Anita E. Woolfolk*

Clearly, parts of this excerpt are factual. The first sentence is no doubt accurate. As educated readers of this textbook, education students probably have heard and used the term *hyperactivity*. Exceptions may exist, but on the whole we can accept the statement as a fact not worth disputing.

And the second sentence, too, is a fact. A check in educational literature over the past few decades would confirm the writer's point. The word *hyperactive* rarely appeared, if at all, in descriptions of children thirty to forty years ago.

The last sentence in this textbook excerpt, however, is the writer's opinion. "Today, if anything, the term is applied too often and too widely" is not a fact. Many educators would agree that the term *hyperactivity* is too unscientific to describe a child's behavior. And hyperactive as a group label can become a dumping ground for too many children who do not follow conventional behavior styles.

However, some educators and parents would dispute Woolfolk's point here. With a label like hyperactive, special children may receive special, extra support from the teacher and the school. Using the term even loosely might identify students who otherwise might escape notice. And a teacher who knows how to deal with children who display restlessness and inattention might deal well with a small group of youngsters with similar behaviors.

The point here is that the view that the term *hyperactivity* is applied too often and too widely is open to discussion.

As a reader, bring a critical eye to the passages you read. Be aware that not all statements in textbooks are facts. To be a critical reader, you have to know how to discern fact from opinion and to question opinions by considering further information, facts, and points of view.

In this selection from a marketing text, note the balance of fact and opinion regarding the issue of "gray marketing." The columns after the piece identify some of the facts and opinions that the writer presents.

Few Black and White Issues in Gray Marketing

Sometimes referred to as diversion, gray marketing occurs when products are diverted from distribution channels selected and authorized by manufacturers to unauthorized dealers. Although the phrase *gray marketing* may evoke images of shadowy deals taking place in back alleys, the practice is a legal and growing one, and it involves genuine, trademarked products. Experts estimate that retail sales of gray market goods add up to about $10 billion a year. Gray marketing proponents insist that there is nothing underhanded about it and value the 10 to 15 percent price reduction that consumers enjoy on gray market items. Those who oppose gray marketing counter that the practice is improper and borders on the illegal.

Gray marketing is practiced both domestically and internationally. Within the United States, big retailers take advantage of volume discounts by purchasing goods in large quantities and reselling them to smaller retailers at lower prices than the manufacturers offer. Wholesale distributors sell products to unauthorized distributors. In both cases, goods are diverted from authorized marketing channel members. The question arises, is it fair that authorized dealers in the marketing channel lose sales because of gray marketers' actions?

At the international level, gray marketing occurs when global products sold in the United States are not brought in by the authorized importers. In this situation, authorized importers are forced to compete with unauthorized ones, which can sell goods at lower prices. Aside from the issue of unfair competition, there is the question of the quality of gray market goods and services. Although customers are happy to get a bargain, they may not be as pleased if the products they buy differ physically or in quality from what they expected, or if service and warranty protection are unsatisfactory.

In the prestige fragrance business and in the computer industry, the ethics of gray marketing are raising particular concern. Sold increasingly in discount outlets at dramatically reduced prices, gray market fragrances are decreasing the profits of both manufacturers and authorized importers of high-end designer perfumes. With respect to computers, customers run certain risks when buying from gray market dealers. Many manufacturers—IBM and Compaq among others—will not honor a warranty unless a machine was purchased from an authorized dealer. Furthermore, gray marketers often add off-brand internal components, such as disk drives, to name brand computers. To make sure that they are getting the product and the service they are looking for, experts recommend that prospective buyers call the manufacturer to check on the dealer's authorization.

Opponents of gray marketing are launching an assault on gray marketers. To prevent consumer confusion and deception, they are lobbying Congress to enact laws requiring labeling of gray market imports. A U.S. Court of Appeals recently ruled that the U.S. Customs Service must block importation of gray market Shield soap and Sunlight dishwashing detergent because these British-made versions differ in composition and looks from their American-made Lever Bros. counterparts.

Regardless of questions of legality or fairness, gray marketing is not going to disappear. Lower wholesale costs translate into lower retail costs, which translate into lower prices for customers. By eliminating gray marketing, the government would drastically limit the number of discounted products available to consumers. The bottom line is that, to get products for considerably lower prices, many consumers are willing to take a chance on getting lower quality and poorer service.

— *William M. Pride and O. C. Ferrell*

Facts	Opinions
• In gray marketing, products are taken from authorized to unauthorized dealers.	• There are few black-and-white issues in gray marketing.
• Retail sales of gray market goods add up to almost $10 billion a year.	• There is nothing underhanded about gray marketing.
• By law, U.S. Customs must prevent the import of some gray market soaps from Britain.	• Gray marketing is improper and borders on the illegal.

Facts	Opinions
• Many manufacturers will not honor warranties from unauthorized dealers.	• Computer customers run risks in buying from gray market dealers.
• Gray market opponents are lobbying Congress to enact laws requiring labeling of gray market imports.	• Gray marketing is not going to disappear.
	• Prospective buyers should call the manufacturer to check on the dealer's authorization.

Keeping Fact and Opinion Apart

• Look for words that *interpret.* In the first of the following sentences, we have details that describe facts—without any evaluation of these facts. In the second sentence, the writer interprets the details for us.

1. The man leaning against the fence had brown eyes, and his black hair touched his shoulders.
2. A handsome man leaned against the fence.

It's somebody's opinion that the man is handsome. Other words that interpret—there are countless examples—are *pretty, ugly, safe, dangerous, evil, attractive, well dressed, good,* and so on.

• Look for words that can serve as clues to statements of opinion. Some words like *probably, perhaps, usually, often, sometimes,* and *on occasion* are used to limit a statement of fact and to indicate the possibility of other opinions. Other words— *I believe, I think, in my opinion, I feel, I suggest—* say clearly that an opinion follows.

- Before you accept a statement of fact and before you agree with a statement of opinion, question the credibility of the writer. Is she reliable? Why should you take her word?
- Test the writer's opinion by asking whether a different opinion is possible. You do not have to agree with the different opinion (or with the writer's for that matter). You just have to be able to see if there is another point of view.
- Some writers include statements from other writers or authorities to illustrate their own ideas. Make sure that you can tell the source of any statement that appears in what you read.

10b Evidence

Sometimes when writers state their opinions, they just assert their points of view without providing any support. In such cases you have no particular reason to believe their opinions unless you trust them as authorities or experts. Any writer (even an "expert") who states opinions without giving supporting evidence probably should not convince you.

More often, writers try to convince readers to share their opinions by presenting various facts or evidence, just as a lawyer presents evidence in a court case to support the opinion that the accused is innocent or guilty of a crime. Just as a jury must evaluate the evidence carefully to decide whether to accept a lawyer's opinion about the accused, so must you evaluate the evidence presented in what you read to decide whether to accept a writer's opinion.

Evaluating Evidence: Questions to Ask Yourself

- Can the facts be trusted?
- Are the facts given objectively?
- Do the facts really support the opinion being expressed?
- Are the facts relevant to the point being made?
- Have unfavorable or negative points been left out?
- Do the facts prove the writer's opinion, or do they only suggest that the opinion is reasonable?

If two writers give opposite opinions, you should judge which one gives the better evidence. Whose facts are more reliable, are more complete, are expressed more objectively? Whose facts support the opinion more fully?

Many times, writers try to convince you to share their opinions. They may use all their persuasive skills to try to make you believe that tall people make better presidents, or that Michael Jackson is the greatest male vocalist, or even that people who use crack should be jailed. Only a careful reader can avoid falling for an emotional or poorly reasoned argument.

10c   The Writer's Technique

An important way to develop critical skills is to be aware of the writer's technique in any selection you read. Once you know what the writer is doing with his or her material—once you know the effect he or she is trying to create—you can judge more fairly and clearly what is said.

10c(1) *Style*

In general, *style* is the way a writer picks words and puts them together. Style usually tells you who the writer expects to read the work. If the sentences are long and the words are difficult, the writer expects an educated reader. If the language is rich in slang expressions and current phrases, the writer is talking to a more general group. If the words are very technical, the writer is aiming for a special audience that knows the language of the subject being discussed. Some writers pick words with deep emotional appeal in order to urge their readers to act. Other writers choose a more impartial style.

A writer who wants to convince you of how urgent a problem is might use short statements so that as you read along, you become wrapped up in the fast pace. During World War II, Winston Churchill said, "We shall fight on the beaches, we shall fight on the landing grounds, we shall fight in the fields and in the streets, we shall fight in the hills; we shall never surrender." Here he used repetition and short statements effectively to show how committed England was to keep fighting. If he had said, "We shall fight them on the beaches and in the streets and never surrender," the basic message would have been the same, but the style would not have fired his listeners' patriotism.

10c(2) *Tone*

Tone is the attitude a writer takes toward a subject. Writers can express, for example, respect, hatred, anger, impatience, humor, or irony.

Oscar Wilde was asked by a judge during his trial, "Are you trying to show contempt for this court?" and Wilde replied, "On the contrary, I'm trying to conceal it." The tone of his response was much more effective than if he had said, "Yes, I am."

10c(3) *Mood*

Mood is a state of mind or feeling at a particular time. Often writers create a mood so that they can make you respond in a certain way.

Edgar Allan Poe said that sibilants (words that contain the *s* sound, like *snake, sinister,* and *shadow*) help create a mysterious mood, and he used sibilants often: "And then did we, the seven, start from our seats in horror, and stand trembling, and shuddering and aghast."

10c(4) *Purpose*

Writers write for a *reason.* Some want to give information. Some want to persuade you to believe something. Others try to push you into taking some action related to a subject of deep meaning to them. Some writers write to amuse or entertain.

Advertising is a good example of writing with a purpose—that is, writing to make you buy a certain product. Another example is editorials in newspapers. Editorials aim at gaining public support for a political position.

10c(5) *Point of View*

Deeply held beliefs and ideas often determine how a writer looks at a given subject. In this sense, *point of view* means "opinions" or "attitudes," although there are a number of other meanings that make it a complex term to use. Our concern here is for the way a writer's own interests and beliefs influence the writing we read. A communist, for example, would look at the Cuban government in a very different way from someone who believes in democracy. A Catholic would not look at religious ceremonies in the same way as a Protestant or a Jew. A black person might have much stronger views on the treatment of sickle-cell anemia than a white person. Sometimes a point of view forces an author to *slant* the writing. Slanted writing leans toward one way of looking at a problem and leaves out ideas that might challenge the slanted view.

Of course, these techniques often blend together. Style and tone are often impossible to separate, and both clearly relate to purpose and point of view. Also, the writer's style often creates a mood. The point in seeing a writer's technique is to notice that what a writer says relates to *how* the writer says it.

10d Techniques That Twist the Truth

As a critical reader, you have to be able to judge unfair writing. Sometimes a piece of writing will not use truthful methods if its purpose is to force you to have a certain opinion about a subject. *Propaganda* (particular ideas forced on the public by organizations with special interests) often develop through the use of unfair writing and logic. Any information that leaves out or alters facts in order to press a special point of view is called *biased, prejudiced,* or *slanted.*

Be on your guard against propaganda. Try to recognize the following methods of propaganda:

■ The writer uses words for emotional effect: *stoner, liberal, nerd, fence-sitter, racist,* for example. Look for emotionally charged words and words that have special connotations (See section **15c**.)

- The writer tries to combine a famous person's name with an idea or product so that people who like the person will like the idea or product too.

  Michael Jordan drinks Gatorade.

- The writer quotes a famous person who approves of or agrees with an idea so that the reader will approve of it too.

  Jacques Martin, the famous French chef, says, "Margarine is just as good as butter." Why are *you* still using butter?

- The writer says that everyone is doing something (or thinking in a certain way), so you should do it too.

  Every farmer, every hard-working city resident knows the dangers of the welfare system.

- The writer uses very positive words in regard to an idea, presenting only general statements rather than specific facts.

  Drivers love this stunning, efficient, and completely safe automobile. Add a bit of sunshine to your life—take a ride in a glamorous, high-fashion car!

- The writer "stacks the deck," a technique that presents only facts that tend to make you agree with the message.

  There's nothing wrong with drinking before driving. Not one person at our party got hurt on the way home—and believe me, not too many people there were sober!

- The writer uses negative terms to refer to a person or product.

  Only a nitwit like Lorna would buy an imported car. Those things look like wind-up toys.

We can see the effect of slanted writing in the following statements:

- What's the use of working? Your money goes to pay taxes and your cheating landlord. And you break your back to make the boss rich.
- Look, you do the best you can. Taxes are high and so is rent. But if you do not work, you give up your pride and the few comforts you have. Of course, the boss has to make a fair profit from your work; otherwise, you would not be hired. You just have to live on what is left over.
- Every American should be proud to work and support the system. Your taxes go to making this country great. And by helping the landowners and the factory owners make money, you are strengthening the backbone of the nation. Hard work makes good Americans.

The first of the three versions is slanted against work by telling only part of the story and by name-calling—making it appear that everybody is out to take advantage of the poor worker. The third version slants the case in the opposite direction by "stacking the deck" in favor of those who benefit from the worker's labor, by using only positive language, and by pressuring the reader to follow a group. Only the second version gives a balanced view, expressed truthfully.

APPLICATIONS: Your Courses

Read a brief selection in one of your textbooks. Make a list of some of the writer's opinions and the supporting evidence provided.

Unit Three

The Basic Study Skills

11

Using SQ3R

SQ3R is a technique or method that helps you understand what you read. It gives you a useful series of steps that can improve your comprehension, particularly in reading textbooks.

The letters stand for the following activities:

- **S** Survey
- **Q** Question
- **R** Read
- **R** Recite
- **R** Review

11a Survey

Survey means the same as *preview*. Its purpose is to give you information about what you are reading *before* you actually begin. When you survey, you do the following:

- Read the sentences that introduce the chapter
- Read the main headings and the subheadings (look for **boldface** or *italic* print)
- Look at the illustrations and photographs and read the captions (sentences that explain the pictures)
- Read the checklists and the questions at the end of the selection
- Read the introductory sentences at the beginning of the chapter

In surveying, don't read all the material. Your purpose is *not* to read the complete piece. You want an overview. Take only a few minutes to survey.

Survey

* Read introductory sentences
✓ Read titles and headings (see bold and italic print)
● Read activity at end of selection

Note survey elements you should use with the sample selection below from an English text.

 ## Giving a Talk

Giving a talk or a speech might bring butterflies to your stomach, make your knees knock and your palms moist, and give you a dry mouth. People who normally have no trouble talking often search for words when they are speaking in front of an audience.

How can you overcome your nervousness and be a good speaker? Remembering these five Ps should help—Prepare, Plan, and Practice, Practice, Practice.

Prepare

1. Choose a topic that is interesting to *you.*
2. Choose a topic that you can research if necessary.
3. If appropriate, add humorous or interesting details or personal stories that will keep your audience interested.

Plan

1. Be sure that you know exactly what you want to say. Make notes or an outline on note cards or slips of paper that you can look at during your talk. Write on your cards only key words that will help you recall your main points and details. You do not want to read your speech.

2. If you are using illustrations or pictures, be sure they are large enough for your audience to see.
3. Ask your family or friends to set aside some time for you to practice your talk in front of them.

Practice

1. Find a quiet place to practice your talk out loud.
2. Read over your notes until you have them almost memorized. Then practice your talk by just glancing at your note cards occasionally. Find the key word, and look up again as you continue with your talk.
3. Practice in front of a mirror so you can see how you look. Your hands are busy with your note cards, but how are you standing? Are you rocking back and forth? Are you pacing like a caged lion? Try standing with your feet slightly apart so that you are comfortable. If you feel yourself getting tense, take a deep breath, and relax.
4. Listen to yourself as you practice out loud. Are you talking loudly enough without shouting? Are you stressing your main points and details? Let your voice show your feelings. Look at one or two spots while you practice. When you give your talk, replace these spots with actual people.
5. Practice in front of your family and friends. Time yourself. If you are over or under your time limit, speed up or slow down or change the length of your talk. Practice using your illustrations. Ask for comments when you finish.

If you follow the five Ps, you will feel confident in front of your audience. You will know that your talk is interesting and that your presentation is strong. Try to enjoy yourself.

Activity

Write notes or a short outline for a five-minute talk on one of the following topics, or choose one of your own.

a strange pet I would like to own
my favorite activity
somewhere I would like to visit

— *John Stewig and Shirley Haley-James*

11b   Question

In the SQ3R process, the *Q* for *question* means that you actually produce your own questions. You identified the main headings and the subheadings when you surveyed. Now look again at the headings (usually in boldface or italic print) and turn each one into a question. Write the question down.

For example, look at the headings taken from the selection "Giving a Talk" and the sample questions prepared from the headings.

Headings	Questions Made from the Headings
Giving a Talk	What steps should I take before giving a talk?
Prepare	How do I prepare for a talk?
Plan	How can I plan correctly for a talk?
Practice	How can I practice the talk effectively?
Activity	What activity will prepare me for the talk?

11c   Read

The first *R, read,* means that now you read the selection from one heading to the next heading and stop before going on. While you read, try to find the answer to the question that you've made up from the heading—from the *Q* step in SQ3R.

Reading in this way keeps you focused on segments of the text. When you read the sentences from one heading to the next, stop before you continue. Your purpose is to read in order to answer the questions you wrote; after you answer each question, continue reading to the next heading. Keep repeating the process. Do not read the whole selection at once.

11d Recite

The second *R*, *recite*, means that after you've read from one heading to the next, you stop reading and try to answer the questions.

Remember:

- Look at the questions that you made up from the heading.
- Read only from one heading to the next.
- Stop before going on.
- Recite the answers to the questions.

After you answer the questions, read down to the next heading. If you can't come up with an answer, read the sentences under the heading again.

11e Review

After you read the whole selection, *review* your reading. *Review* means "look again." Simply go back, read your questions another time, and try to answer them.

This time, however, do not read the material under each heading. Now you're trying to remember what you read, by thinking about each question and giving an answer. If you can't answer a particular question, reread only the material under the heading that will answer your question.

How to Use SQ3R

- **Survey.** Preview the material before you read. (Look at headings, photos, and illustrations, checklists, sentences that introduce chapters, questions.)
- **Question.** Make questions from all the headings and subheadings you found when you surveyed.

Example:

Heading: The Impact of Divorce
Question: What is the impact of divorce on a
   child?

- **Read.** Read the selection from one heading to the next and stop before going on. As you read, try to find answers to the questions you made from the headings.
- **Recite.** Stop reading and answer the questions. After producing answers to your own questions, repeat the process: Read down to the next heading and answer the next questions.
- **Review.** When you finish the reading, go back, read your questions another time, and try again to answer them.

12

Writing for Reading

You can improve your understanding of what you read by using a variety of writing strategies. These strategies include *underlining, highlighting, taking notes, outlining,* and *summarizing.*

12a Underlining and Highlighting

If you underline or highlight the most important ideas and details in a reading assignment, you can rapidly find what you need when you reread the passage. You also can add special marks and comments in the margin about the main ideas and major details you underline. *Annotating*—writing comments and questions in the margins (after reflecting on the text)—can help you remember your thoughts and interpretation of the passage.

A highlighter pen lets you write directly over key words in a passage so that the words stand out in a colored background. When you look back over the page, highlighted words should indicate the major ideas that you found as you read.

A Method for Underlining

- Underline only reading material that belongs to you. Do not mark up library books, borrowed books, or books that belong to your school. Underlining is a personal process. Your underlining may interfere with other readers' use and enjoyment of a book.
- If you use a highlighter, be selective. That is, highlight only essential information.
- Mark the main ideas and the major details differently. Underline the main ideas with a double line and the major details with a single line. Or use a different color highlighter pen for each.
- Find main-idea sentences by following the suggestions in section **4b.** Identify the sentences or parts of sentences that state the main idea of a paragraph. If the main idea is only implied, write your own main-idea sentence in the margin.
- Find major details by following the suggestions in section **5b.** Identify these major details.
- If you use underlining strategies, you can circle key words. Use brackets ([]), asterisks (*), or any other symbol to mark parts that are especially interesting or important to you.
- Write notes or comments to yourself in the margin. The margins are good places to put down your own thoughts as you read. Margin notes can help you connect ideas from different parts of the selection. They can also help you connect a passage with other material you have read, comments your instructor has made, or your own experience.

In the following passage, note how one student used the technique of underlining and making margin notes to highlight important points.

⏷ Where Does Money Come From?

Stages
1. Cattle

From the earliest agricultural times some <u>9000 years ago</u> people used <u>cattle for currency</u>, a practice that has carried into the present in our word "pecuniary," from the Latin *pecus*, meaning "cattle."

2. Metal ingots

<u>Metallic money appeared</u> considerably later, <u>about 2000 B.C.</u>, in the form of bronze ingots, often <u>shaped like cattle</u> and traded on the open market according to their weight. Not only were amulets of cattle infinitely more convenient to exchange than the real thing, but the intrinsic brilliance of the metallic pieces heightened their esthetic appeal. Exchanging money then, however, always required the presence of an honest <u>balance-beam scale</u> and often was accompanied by a fiery dispute when the honesty of one of the parties was impugned.

cheating easy

3. Rare metals

By <u>about 1000 B.C. bronze had been superseded by the purer, rarer</u> metals, <u>silver</u> and <u>gold</u>, and cattle shapes had given way to heads of cats (particularly in Egypt, where cat worship reached obsessional heights), statuettes of rulers, deities, or merely ornamental medallions. These pieces, too, derived their worth from weight, a troublesome standard that would survive only a few hundred years longer.

new shapes

4. Protocoins

The <u>first protocoins were produced by the Lydians of Anatolia about 800 B.C.</u> Made of electrum, a natural <u>alloy of gold</u> containing as much as 35 percent silver, these pieces were crude, <u>bean-shaped ingots</u> that bore a <u>punch-mark signifying their worth</u>, thus obviating the need for a scale.

5. True coins   Around <u>640 B.C., the Lydians began produc-</u> <u>ing the first true coins</u> (the word "coin" is a Latin derivative from *cuneus,* or "wedge"). They were made by a smith <u>hammering a</u> <u>punch through a sheet of electrum as it lay on</u> <u>his anvil. Being a malleable alloy,</u> electrum made possible the imprinting of a figure of a man or an animal on the coin's face; a particu- lar relief signified a coin's value, which almost immediately led to cheating on the ratio of gold to silver in the currency.

— Charles Panati

12b Taking Notes

Identify the main ideas and major details in your reading; then write them down in an organized list. Indent the less important information underneath the more important, so that you see how the parts of the reading fit together.

The following notes are based on the passage about the origin of coin money (pages 134–135).

First money—cattle, 9000 years ago
First metal money—bronze ingots in shape of cattle,
   2000 B.C.
     Had to be weighed.
By 1000 B.C. silver and gold in shape of cat heads
800 B.C., first protocoins of gold alloy
     Bean-shaped ingots with punchmark of value
640 B.C., first real coin by Lydians
     Value given by figure punched on
Electrum makes imprinting possible

These notes help bring out the time-order organiza- tion of the passage. Each main point lists a new stage in the development of coin money.

A Method for Taking Notes

- Find the main ideas following the suggestions in section **4b.** Write these main ideas down on notebook paper, starting at the left margin of the paper. You may copy the entire main-idea sentence as it appears in the reading, shorten it, or put the idea in your own words. You can even jot down just a few key phrases from the printed text, as long as they capture the main idea.

- Find the major details, following the suggestions in section **5b.** List them opposite or beneath your notes on the main ideas. Again, you don't need to copy whole sentences. Phrases or words will do. Your own wording of the printed text will do, as long as your notes capture the important facts or ideas.

- Use abbreviations, but make sure you will be able to understand their meanings when you return to the notes, weeks or months later.

- Add your own comments and thoughts in the margins or in a special section at the bottom of the page. These comments will help you think through the importance of the material or highlight its relation to other reading you have done.

- You can use a similar method for taking notes during course lectures. Make sure you keep up with the lecture. Don't get so caught up in taking notes that you stop listening. If you find the lecturer getting too far ahead of you, stop writing and start listening. If you skip a few lines, you can always complete your notes later from memory or from a friend's notes. During lectures, avoid fussing over the spelling and exact wording of your notes. You can always check the dictionary later.

12c Outlining

Outlining is an organized form of note taking. In an outline a system of numbering and indenting entries helps organize ideas by level of importance. The main ideas begin at the left margin, numbered with Roman numerals. Supporting ideas, indented under the main ideas, are marked with capital letters. Less important material is indented further and given Arabic numerals (and then lowercase letters at the next level).

An outline arrangement of your notes lets you see at a glance how the key ideas relate to one another and how the writer backs up the main points.

How to Make Successful Outlines

- List only main ideas as main headings.
- Relate all subheadings to the main heading they follow.
- Make sure all the headings in a series fit together logically.
- Make sure the headings are clearly different, that they don't cover the same material. If there is too much overlap, you should reorganize the outline.
- Make sure that whenever you break down a heading, you have at least two subheadings.
- Include everything important that appears in the selection you are outlining.
- Use whole sentences, phrases, or just single words, as long as the entries convey the information and are easy to understand. If you use sentences in one part, however, you should use sentences throughout the outline.
- Indent all items correctly.
- Put a period after each letter or number.

The following sample outline is based on the passage on the origin of coin money on pages 134–135.

I. First currency—cattle
  A. 9000 years ago
  B. Pecuniary—from Latin word for "cattle"
II. First metal money, in form of metal ingots
  A. Bronze used first
  B. Shaped like cattle
  C. 2000 B.C.
    1. Pretty and convenient
    2. Exchanged by weight
      a. Required honest scale
      b. Led to disputes
  D. Bronze replaced by rarer metals
    1. 1000 B.C.
    2. Gold, silver
    3. Shaped like cat heads
III. Coins with worth punched on
  A. First protocoins by Lydians
    1. About 800 B.C.
    2. Gold alloy
    3. Bean-shaped ingots
  B. First true coins by Lydians
    1. 640 B.C.
    2. Gold alloy
    3. Value in relief figure
    4. Cheating on gold to silver ratio

12d Summarizing

Summaries are brief statements that fit together a selection's most important facts and ideas in shorter versions of the original passages. In order to summarize a paragraph, first read it to identify all its important ideas and facts. Underline key words and phrases. Cross out any information that is not major.

Then write a single sentence as a summary and have it include all the important material you have identified. One brief sentence can often show the relations among several important parts of a paragraph.

Compare the next paragraph with the various single-sentence summaries that follow it.

> Although several early societies experimented with paper currency—most notably the Chinese during the 1st millennium B.C.—coins of silver and gold predominated as the major form of exchange. The reasons were understandable enough: coins were far more durable than paper and less likely to be destroyed by fire, and coins contained the very precious metals that made money worth its salt. It required a leap of both imagination and of courage to establish a form of currency that was only backed by a precious metal but of itself was intrinsically worthless.
>
> — *Charles Panati*

One approach would be to look at the opening sentence as a source for your own summary sentence:

> Although several early societies experimented with paper currency—most notably the Chinese during the 1st millennium B.C.—coins of silver and gold predominated as the major form of exchange.

A few eliminations and some rewriting creates a compact summary based on the opening sentence:

> Coins of silver and gold predominated as the major form of exchange over early experiments with paper currency.

You can produce an even more accurate summary than the last example by taking key ideas from the *entire* paragraph, not just the opening topic sentence. Write them in your own words. In the original paragraph, the key information is not just that coins were the major form of exchange. We also learn *why* coins predominated (remained the leading elements). A good summary would include that information:

> Because silver and gold were more durable, less flammable, and more intrinsically valuable, they predominated over early paper money.

When you summarize a passage of several paragraphs or longer, you can produce one sentence to summarize the information of each important paragraph. However, you may want to combine related information from several summary sentences into one sentence. You may also devote two or more sentences to summarize long, important paragraphs. Or you may choose not to summarize paragraphs that serve as transitions, repeat information you've already summarized, or provide lengthy illustrations.

In the summary of the passage on the origin of coin money from pages 134–135, the writer combined important facts and ideas and eliminated less important information. Look at how combining sentences and using words such as *because* and *then* bring out the connections between ideas. Also, the clustering of sentences in separate paragraphs helps bring out the differences between ingots and coins.

The use of cattle as currency, dating back 9000 years, was replaced in 2000 B.C. by bronze ingots in the shape of cattle. Because these pretty, convenient ingots were traded according to weight, disputes occurred over the honesty of the weighing. Gold and silver ingots in the shape of cat heads replaced the bronze ingots by 1000 B.C.

The first protocoins, produced by the Lydians around 800 B.C. out of a gold alloy, had a punchmark showing their worth. The Lydians in 640 B.C. produced the first real coins with a figure on them signifying their value and leading to cheating on the coins' ratio of gold to silver.

An opening sentence giving the main idea helps tie a long summary together. Show the relations between sentences by having their ideas follow one another logically and by using connecting words and phrases to stress how the ideas fit together. For a summary that requires more than five or six sentences, cluster related summary sentences together in separate paragraphs. The paragraph breaks should show the main divisions of the author's original ideas.

Summaries help you remember the most important information in a reading, and how the writer put the ideas together, by getting you to restate the information in your own way.

For study purposes a summary is usually about a quarter of the length of the original text. When you write a summary of a long selection, make your summary shorter in proportion to the original, perhaps as short as one-tenth the length.

How to Prepare a Summary

- Carefully read the entire passage. Make sure you understand all the vocabulary and concepts. Check a dictionary when necessary.
- Underline or list separately the main ideas and major details of the reading.
- Select the main idea of the passage as the most important idea of the summary. This will usually be the first sentence of your summary.
- Rewrite the facts and ideas into sentences that show the connections among them. If you combine several facts and ideas in one sentence, make their connections clear. Be careful not to combine information without any logical connection.

- Avoid repeating unnecessary words from the original material. Leave out all but the most important details.
- Present ideas and information in an organized way that reflects the meaning of the original version. Don't jump suddenly from one point to the next. Use connecting words like *first, second, on the other hand, because,* and *although* to show how your summary statements fit together.

12e Your Opinion: Keeping a Journal

In order to evaluate fairly the ideas expressed in a piece of writing, you need to become aware of your own opinions and reactions. One way to sort out your thinking is to keep a reading journal, a kind of diary of your thoughts about your reading. As you read, try to find time to write out your thoughts and reactions. State whether or not you liked or agreed with the passage and why. Give reasons for your objections to what you've read. If the reading reminds you of something you have experienced, describe that experience and how it is related to the reading. If other facts you know or ideas you hold support the writer's opinions, discuss them. If you dislike the writer's attitude or manner of looking at the subject, explain exactly what is wrong with the writer's approach.

Write down your ideas and develop them in your journal. Do not be satisfied with expressing an opinion in a single sentence or two. Explain your ideas further, give examples, indicate why you feel as you do. Think your thoughts through in any way that strikes you.

Read the following selection from a textbook in world civilizations. It describes the reasons for the spread of the bubonic plague.

In 1291 Genoese sailors had opened the Straits of   1
Gibraltar to Italian shipping by defeating the
Moroccans. Then, shortly after 1300, important
advances were made in the design of Italian merchant ships. A square rig was added to the main-
mast, and ships began to carry three masts instead
of just one. Additional sails better utilized wind
power to propel the ship. The improved design
permitted year-round shipping for the first time,
and Venetian and Genoese merchant ships could
sail the dangerous Atlantic coast even in the winter months. With ships continually at sea, the rats
that bore the disease spread rapidly beyond the
Mediterranean to Atlantic and North Sea ports.

Around 1331 the bubonic plague broke out in   2
China. In the course of the next fifteen years, mer-
chants, traders, and soldiers carried the disease
across the Asian caravan routes until in 1346 it
reached the Crimea in southern Russia. From there
the plague had easy access to the Mediterranean
lands and western Europe.

In October 1347, Genoese ships brought the   3
plague to Messina, from which it spread throughout Sicily. Venice and Genoa were hit in January
1348, and from the port of Pisa the disease spread
south to Rome and east to Florence and all
Tuscany. By late spring, southern Germany was
attacked. Frightened French authorities chased a
galley bearing the disease from the port of
Marseilles, but not before plague had infected the
city, from which it spread to Languedoc and Spain.
In June 1348, two ships entered the Bristol
Channel and introduced it into England. All
Europe felt the scourge of this horrible disease.

Although by the fourteenth century urban   4
authorities from London to Paris to Rome had

begun to try to achieve a primitive level of sanitation, urban conditions remained ideal for the spread of disease. Narrow streets filled with mud, refuse, and human excrement were as much cesspools as thoroughfares. Dead animals and sore-covered beggars greeted the traveler. Houses whose upper stories projected over the lower ones eliminated light and air. And extreme overcrowding was commonplace. When all members of an aristocratic family lived and slept in one room, it should not be surprising that six or eight persons in a middle-class or poor household slept in one bed—if they had one. Closeness, after all, provided warmth. Houses were beginning to be constructed of brick, but many remained of wood, clay, and mud. A determined rat had little trouble entering such a house.

Standards of personal hygiene remained frightfully low. Since water was considered dangerous, partly for good reasons, people rarely bathed. Skin infections, consequently, were common. Lack of personal cleanliness, combined with any number of temporary ailments such as diarrhea and the common cold, naturally weakened the body's resistance to serious disease. Fleas and body lice were universal afflictions: everyone from peasants to archbishops had them. One more bite did not cause much alarm. But if that nibble came from a bacillus-bearing flea, an entire household or area was doomed.

— *John McKay*

Now read this reading journal entry that a student wrote about the selection.

This sounds really disgusting. I don't know what I would do if I was alive back then. Maybe I'd go live in the woods by myself for a few years until everything was cool again. I can't believe people actually killed the cats that could have saved them. That seems totally stupid. But I know there was very little medical knowledge at the time, so people were using superstition. There are scary diseases today like AIDS, the Ebola virus, and flesh-eating bacteria, but at least medicine understands how they are caused and may even find a cure for them someday. The plague seems as bad as AIDS only in super-fast-forward. At least people who get AIDS can hang around for a little while. The plague killed people in a couple of days. That's hardly even enough time to say goodbye. Although I guess not too many people would want to hang with you if you had the plague. I just realized that we think we're so much better than people in the Middle Ages, but when it comes to handling other people's sickness, we're really not that different. People today don't know how to act around people with AIDS. Some neighborhoods and schools won't let people with AIDS in them, and many people don't want to talk about the disease at all.

The writer of this journal entry didn't just summarize the material he read, but started to think about his reactions to the issues of disease raised in the selection. Notice, also, how the student writer related the situations described in the selection to his own experiences and feelings about illness.

13

Understanding Exam Questions

The two basic kinds of exam questions are *short-answer* (or objective questions) and *essay* questions. Short-answer questions test whether you know specific pieces of information and can solve straightforward problems that have a single answer. Essay questions test not only whether you know specific information but also how well you understand and can apply that information to a subject.

13a Prepare for Examinations

Prepare for examinations by keeping up with class lectures and assigned readings by underlining or highlighting, taking notes, outlining, and summarizing (see Chapter 12). The following steps will help you review course material and focus your studying for exams.

How to Prepare for Exams

- *Get an overview of the entire course.* Look over a syllabus, the table of contents of your text, a list of lectures, an assignment sheet, or any material distributed at the beginning of the course. Outline or list all the major topics covered in

---

class and in the readings. Look for patterns and themes emphasized throughout the semester.

- *Think about the overview.* The overview should help you determine what is important and what kinds of exam questions an instructor is likely to ask. The overview can also help you sort out which topics are fairly clear and fresh in your mind and which topics are unclear, calling for a long, thorough review of all your notes and study tools.

- *Schedule your study time.* Divide your available time according to the importance of each topic and how well you know the topic. Don't waste time memorizing minor facts; spend your study time on the most important material.

- *Study the material topic by topic, in an orderly way.* Combine in outline form the key concepts and facts from both class and reading assignments. The more you see the logical connections among the many facts and concepts, the more you will remember and the better you will understand the material.

13b Short-Answer Questions

Read the directions carefully to help you schedule your testing time and guide your decisions and to learn the following pieces of vital information.

■ *Discover how many questions you have to answer.* Knowing how much work you have ahead of you will help you plan your time.

■ *Find out whether you have any choices.* If you have choices, make sure you understand and follow the directions exactly. If, in the first part of the exam, you are supposed to answer only ten out of twenty questions, but you answer all twenty anyway, you have wasted time. The last ten answers will not count on your test results. If in the second part you are supposed to answer twenty out of twenty-five questions, but you answer only fifteen, you will lose credit for five questions.

■ *Pay attention to how much time you have.* You may have one block of time for the whole exam, or you may have smaller blocks for each part. In either case, do not waste too much time on a single question and then rush through all the remaining questions.

■ *Determine how many points each question is worth.* If some questions are worth more points than others, spend more time on the more valuable questions. Also notice whether incorrect answers count against you. If there is no penalty, you should make your best guess, even if you are not sure of the answer. But if there is a penalty, you may be better off leaving some questions blank rather than making wild guesses.

■ *Know beforehand what extra materials you are allowed.* You may be allowed to use the textbook, a calculator, your notes, or scrap paper. Usually the instructor will let you know ahead of time which materials are permitted so that you can bring them with you. If you do not bring the extra materials allowed, you are putting yourself at a serious disadvantage.

■ *Find out where to record your answers.* Sometimes you may be allowed to fill in or circle the answer on the question itself, but more often special places are provided for the answers. If you have to fill in spaces on a machine-scored sheet, be sure to mark the spaces neatly and clearly. If you have to use a special pencil, be sure that you have one and that you use it. If your answer is in the wrong place or cannot be read, it will do you no good.

■ *Notice what type or types of questions are included.* Different types of questions require different types of answers.

Fill-in questions ask you to write a missing word or phrase in a blank space within a statement. When filling in the blank, try to use the exact term used in class or in your textbook.

True-false questions require you to state whether or not a particular statement is correct. In true-false questions, words such as *all, most, some, none, always, probably, never, more,* and *less* are very important. In *modified true-false* questions, you may have a third or fourth choice, such as *uncertain* or *not enough data.* Make sure you know all the possible ways of answering before writing down an answer.

Matching questions provide you with lists of information. You must then indicate, next to each item on one list, the related item from the other list. Sometimes one column contains extra items, so that some will be left over. In answering matching questions, you should fill in the easiest answers first, crossing out items as you use them. This will make the unused choices easier for you to see.

Multiple-choice questions usually ask you to choose the best single answer out of four or five choices. But be careful: Sometimes the directions will tell you to choose the *worst* answer or the one item that does *not* apply. The directions may also give you the choice of *none of the above* or *all of the above.* In multiple-choice questions, make sure that you read all the possible answers before writing down your choice. The second choice may sound like a possible answer, but the fifth choice may turn out to be the most precise and therefore the correct answer. If you do not spot the correct answer the first time you read through the choices, you may be able to eliminate some clearly wrong answers.

13c   Essay Questions

Here too, follow directions very carefully. Before you begin to write, take the time to read each question thoroughly and analyze exactly what the question asks.

In reading an essay question, look for the *subject* and the *task.*

The *subject* is the event, process, concept, or other piece of information that the question asks you to discuss. Look at this question from a history exam:

> Evaluate Winston Churchill's role as a leader during World War II.

The subject of the question is Winston Churchill and, more specifically, his leadership during World War II. You would be wrong if you discussed Franklin D. Roosevelt's leadership. You would also be wrong if you discussed Churchill's leadership after the war or during World War I. You must stay within the specific limits of an essay question.

Some questions have two or more subjects. For example, you may be asked to compare or relate two separate ideas. Look at the following question, also from a history exam:

> Compare Winston Churchill's power to inspire the British in the early days of World War II with Franklin D. Roosevelt's inability to alert Americans to the dangers of Hitler during the same period.

In this question you must compare two subjects, which means that you must discuss each one in your answer. If you discuss only one, you are providing only half the information asked for.

The *task* is what you are asked to do with the information. The task usually appears in a *key question word*, often the first word of the question. In the first example, the task was *to evaluate;* in the second, the task was *to compare.* These tasks require different kinds of answers.

The following list of key question words defines and gives examples of the different tasks often demanded in an essay examination.

agree, disagree, comment on, criticize, evaluate	Give your opinion about a book, quotation, or statement. If the question says *agree or disagree,* you must express either a positive or a negative opinion. If the question says *comment on, criticize,* or *evaluate,* your answer can include both positive and negative points.
	"The first six weeks of life are the most important period in a child's emotional development. *Agree* or *disagree.*"

analyze	Break down a topic into all its parts. Be sure to include all the parts and to tell what makes each part different from the others.
	"Analyze the role that computers play in simplifying registration procedures at your college."
compare	Show how two subjects are both alike and different. Be sure to discuss each subject and give both likenesses and differences.
	"Compare laptop computers with desktop personal computers (PC's)."
contrast	Show only the differences between two subjects. Be sure to talk about each one.
	"Contrast the nervous system of a flatworm with the nervous system of a frog."
define	Give the exact meaning of a word, phrase, or concept. Show how what you are defining is different from everything else of its type. Cite examples.
	"Define the word *honor* using examples from your own life that show how you behaved in an honorable way."
describe,	Tell what happened, what a sub-
discuss	ject looks like, or what a subject is.
	"Describe the conditions on the ships that brought slaves to

America. Then *discuss* one rebellion that took place on a slave ship."

explain why
Give the main reasons why an event mentioned happened or happens.

"*Explain why* ocean tides are not high at the same time every night and *why* they are not always the same height."

illustrate
Give one or more examples to support a general statement. Be sure to relate each example to the general statement.

"*Illustrate* the importance of freedom with examples of actions that you as a citizen of a free society can take that a citizen of a dictatorship cannot."

interpret
Explain the meaning of facts given. The question may specify a method of interpretation you must use. Be sure to go beyond just repeating the facts.

"In 1910 Farmtown, Kansas, had 502 farm workers, 37 other blue-collar workers, and 13 white-collar workers. In 1975 the same town had 153 farm workers, 289 other blue-collar workers, and 86 white-collar workers. *Interpret* these statistics in light of national labor trends during this period."

justify, prove
Give reasons to show why a statement is true.

"The Industrial Revolution allowed some people to accumulate great wealth. *Justify* this statement, using material you studied this semester."

list, state   Itemize important points. Be sure to list all the items asked for in the question. Do not give examples unless they are requested.

"*List* the conditions that trigger a response from the body's immune system."

outline, review, summarize   Give all the main points of a quotation, book, or theory. You do not have to include minor points.

"*Outline* the contribution that immigrants made to the quality of American life in the years between 1865 and 1925."

relate   Show how one object has an effect on another. Be sure to identify the connection between them.

"*Relate* the evolution of the horse to the changes in its environment."

trace, list the steps or stages   List a series of important events, leading up to a final item or point. Be sure not to leave any item out or to include more than the question asks for. This type of exam question may refer to historical events, recall a process, or ask for detailed directions.

"*Trace* the development of the modern banking system from its origins in the Renaissance to the eighteenth century."

Answering Essay Questions

- Think about the question. Ask yourself:
  How does the question relate to the course material?
  Can I use any of the important ideas that the instructor emphasized?
  What, from the reading or lectures, would make good examples?
- Plan your essay. On scrap paper list the main points you want to make. Next to each main point note at least one supporting example.
- Make each point clearly.
  — In the opening sentence of your answer, use words from the question. If the question says, "Agree or disagree with the following quotation by Bertrand Russell," you should begin your answer with "I agree (or disagree) with the quotation by Bertrand Russell because. . . ."
  — Begin each of the middle paragraphs with a topic sentence that states one of your major points. Within each middle paragraph, support the major point with reasons and examples.
  — In the conclusion of your essay, relate your answer to one important idea taught in the course.
- Read over the essay you have written. Be sure that all the sentences make sense. Make sure that your meaning is clear. Check that your answer covers each part of the essay question. Make sure that your grammar, sentence structure, and spelling are correct.

Unit Four

Vocabulary

14

Identifying and Remembering New Words

14a How to Find Out What Words Mean

To read well, you need a strong vocabulary. To build a strong vocabulary, you need to read well.

These sentences are a paradox—that is, they seem to express opposite points but, nevertheless, both are true. Together, they state the challenge facing anyone trying to improve reading skills. In order to read confidently, you have to know many words. You have to know how to figure out the meanings for new words that you discover as you read. Yet the best way to expand your knowledge of words is to read often and in varied content areas. Reading and vocabulary are strongly connected. As you improve your skills in one, you improve your skills in the other.

How to Define Difficult Words in Your Readings

- Learn to use the *context*—that is, clues that surrounding sentences sometimes give about the meanings of new words.

- In a word you don't know, look for parts of the word whose meanings you might know.
- Learn the difference between what a word means and what a word suggests or makes you feel.
- Learn the difference between words that mean almost the same thing but have different shades of meaning.
- Learn to use a dictionary so you can find meanings easily.
- Keep a list of words you want to add to your vocabulary.

14b How to Remember New Words

Once you've found the meaning of a new word and you think you understand it, try to make sure that you don't forget it.

How to Remember New Words

- Write the word and its definition often, just for practice.
- Say the word. Learn to pronounce it correctly by using the pronunciation clues in your dictionary.
- Try to learn the word and its meaning the first time you see it.
- Use index cards to study vocabulary. Write the word on one side of the card and its definition on the other side.
- Make up a phrase or a sentence that uses the word in a way you understand.
- Change the ending of the word: Try making it plural; try changing the tense; try adding *ly*.

- Use the word when you talk—in class, on the job, at home.
- Use the word whenever you can in your writing assignments.
- Say the word and its meaning over and over again in your mind.
- Don't try to learn long lists of new words. Study just a few words each day for several days so that you can learn by repeating.

Index Card for
Vocabulary Study

Side One

rickety

Side Two

Meaning
  feeble, shaky

Sentence
  I leaned on the rickety
  table and it fell apart.

APPLICATIONS: Your Courses

From any course you are now taking, identify five new words, determine their meanings, and integrate them into your vocabulary.

15

Building a Strong Vocabulary

15a   Context Clues to Word Meanings

In the second paragraph of Chapter 14 (page 158), you read the word *paradox*. If that word was unfamiliar to you, you still could have figured out its meaning. Look again at the first sentence of the paragraph and at the paragraph that comes just before it.

> To read well, you need a strong vocabulary. To build a strong vocabulary, you need to read well.
>
> These sentences are a paradox—that is, they seem to express opposite points but, nevertheless, both are true.

If you read carefully, you could have defined the word *paradox* from context clues. *Context clues* are hints provided by the words and sentences surrounding the unfamiliar word. The dash (—) and the words *that is* introduce a definition of *paradox*. A paradox is a statement that seems contradictory but is true. If you had checked a dictionary, you would have found a definition quite similar to that one. But you didn't really need a dictionary in this case: Surrounding sentences supplied enough hints for you to guess the meaning of the word *paradox*.

How to Use Sentence Hints to Find Word Meanings

Hint	Example	Explanation
Some sentences set off the definition of a difficult word by means of punctuation.	*Ruminants*, grazing animals such as cows and sheep, are a major cause of erosion in pastures and farming communities.	Commas, dashes —, parentheses (), brackets [].
	Molecules—combinations of atoms —form all chemical compounds.	
Sometimes *helping words*, along with punctuation, provide important clues.	Mary felt *perturbed;* that is, she was greatly disturbed by her sister's actions.	Helping words: *that is, meaning, such as, or, is called.*
Some sentences tell the opposite of what a new word means. From its opposite, you can figure out the meaning of the word.	Parents who constantly spank their children cannot be called *lenient*.	If you are *lenient*, you do not often punish your children. *Merciful* or *gentle* would be a good guess for the meaning of *lenient*. Helping words to show opposites: *not, but, although, however, on the other hand.*

Sometimes you can use your own experiences to figure out the definition of a word.	The *cacophonous* rattling made Maria cover her ears.	A noise that would make you cover your ears would be *unpleasant* or *jarring*.
Sentences before or after a sentence containing a difficult word sometimes explain the meaning of the word.	Mozart gave his first public recital at the age of six. By age thirteen, he had written symphonies and an operetta. He is justly called a child *prodigy*.	It would certainly take a remarkably talented person to do these things. An extraordinary person, then, would be a *prodigy*.
Some sentences are written just to give the definitions of difficult words— words that readers need to know in order to understand what they are reading.	In ancient Greece, most men spent a portion of their day at the *palestra*. This was a public place for exercise and athletics.	The second sentence explains that a *palestra* was a place for exercising and playing sports.
Some sentences give examples of a new word, which allow you to build a definition.	Select a *periodical* from among the following: *People, Time, Reader's Digest*, or *Seventeen*.	The sentence doesn't say that a *periodical* is a magazine, but the examples are magazines.
Some sentences use a word you do know to help explain a word you don't know.	A *formidable* enemy is one to be feared.	*Formidable*— through the sentence clues— means *fearsome* or *dreadful*.

15b   Word-Part Clues to Meaning

Compound Words

Occasionally, two words join to form a new, perhaps unfamiliar, word called a *compound word.* If you look at each part (unit) of the word, though, you can sometimes recognize the new word. Then you can try to understand the meaning. For example, look at these words:

quicksand (quick + sand)
shortfall (short + fall)
cutthroat (cut + throat)
chatterbox (chatter + box)
highbrow (high + brow)

Prefixes, Suffixes, and Roots

Words new to you may contain certain groups of letters that have meanings you can learn. If you don't know what the word itself means, these groups of letters may help you define the word.

When a group of letters with a special meaning appears in front of a word, it is called a *prefix.*

When a group of letters with a special meaning appears at the end of a word, it is called a *suffix.*

The *root* (or *stem*) is the basic part of a word. When we add prefixes or suffixes to certain roots, we create new words. Look at the word *introspective:*

- The root *spect* means "look."
- The prefix *intro* means "within" or "inward."
- The suffix *ive* means "to tend to" or "to lean toward."

If you knew the meanings of these word parts, you might have been able to see that *introspective* means, in a very exact sense, "to tend to look inward."

If you learn key prefixes, roots, and suffixes, you will be able to grasp the meanings of many words without looking them up in a dictionary.

15b(1) *Important Prefixes*

The following prefixes all mean "no" or "not":

Prefix	Meaning	Example
a	not, without	amoral
anti	against	antisocial
il	not	illegal
im	not	immobile
in	not	insensitive
ir	not	irresponsible
mal	badly	malformed
mis	wrongly	misdirected
non	not	nonreturnable
un	not	unattractive

These prefixes all deal with time:

Prefix	Meaning	Example
ante	before	antedated
post	after	postoperative
pre	before	prerequisite

These prefixes deal with numbers:

Prefix	Meaning	Example
auto	self	autograph
bi	two	bifocal
mono	one	monologue
multi	many	multicolored

Prefix	Meaning	Example
poly	many	polygon
tri	three	tripod
uni	one	unicycle

These prefixes deal with placement:

Prefix	Meaning	Example
ab	away from	abnormal
circum	around	circumscribe
com	with, together	committee
de	down from	descend
dis	away	discharge
ex	out of	expel
inter	among	intertwine
per	through	perceive
re	again	rebirth
sub	under	submarine
super	above	supersede
trans	across	transition

15b(2) *Important Roots*

Root	Meaning	Example
cred	believe	credible
equ	equal	equate
fac, fact	do, make	factory
graph	written	monograph
mis, mit	send	missile
mor, mort	die	mortify
nomen	name	nominal
port	carry	portable
pos	place	position
spic, spec	look	spectator
tang	touch	tangible

Root	Meaning	Example
vert	turn	subvert
vid, vis	see	vision
voc	call	vocation

15b(3) *Important Suffixes*

Suffix	Meaning	Example
able ible	able to be	manageable defensible
al ance ence ic	relating to	regal resistance independence heroic
hood ion ism ity ment	state of, quality of	brotherhood union patriotism legality puzzlement
er ite or	one who	writer Mennonite instructor
ful y	full of	wishful soapy

15c Denotation and Connotation

The *denotation* of a word is what the word literally means. *Bicycle*, for instance, means "a two-wheeled vehicle." An *addax* is an animal that is like an antelope and that has two spiral horns.

Many words have other kinds of meaning beyond their dictionary meanings. The word *blue*, for example, denotes "the color of a clear sky." Beyond the denotation of the word, we also can find many other meanings in the name of the color. We usually do not like feeling *blue*, but we may enjoy hearing a great *blues* singer. We would like to have friends who are "true blue," to win a "blue ribbon," and to own "blue-chip stocks." But we might not like being called a "bluenose." As you see, even a simple word naming a color can have a wide range of possible meanings, depending on how it's used. This is what is meant by *connotation*, the implied (suggested) meaning of a word.

Often words with similar denotations have very different connotations. All the words in boldface type below denote a person who is not a male. Yet in each case, the connotation is different.

female   a member of the sex that produces eggs or bears young

woman   an adult female human being

girl a human female who has not matured into womanhood

lady   a woman with refined habits and gentle manners

chick   a degrading slang word for a young woman

Knowing connotations of words helps you understand language more fully than you might otherwise. You can see from the list above, for example, that *female, woman, girl, lady,* and *chick* should not be used interchangeably, even though the words share similar denotations and even though many people ignore the differences among these words. Unless you were commenting on her social behavior, you'd be inaccurate if you referred to a physician who was not a man as a "lady" doctor. (If you *had* to signify the doctor's sex, *woman* would be much more accurate.) And most young women dislike being called *chicks*, although young men talking among themselves might not think twice about using the word.

The more you develop a sense of connotation, the more you will understand how a writer can influence your emotional reactions to words.

15d   Shades of Meaning

Some words, although they seem to mean nearly the same thing, actually mean separate, distinct things. *Boat*, for example, refers to a small craft that is usually open at the top, and *ship* refers to a large seagoing craft. Yet there are many different types of boats and ships, and each type is named by a specific word. Here are a few of them:

barge   a roomy flat-bottomed boat
battleship   a large, heavily armed warship
destroyer   a small fast warship
dinghy   a small rowboat
freighter   a ship for carrying freight
schooner   a large sailing ship
scow   a square-edged barge for carrying garbage or gravel

These words name some kind of unpleasant feeling, but notice how different each word is:

envy   a painful awareness that somebody has something you want
jealousy   hostility toward a rival
suspicion   distrust
resentment   a feeling that someone has wronged you
grudge   a long-lasting resentment
revenge   the desire to hurt someone in return for what he or she has done

malice   the desire to do harm for evil pleasure

The best place to find the shades of meaning of any word is in a dictionary. (See Chapter 14.)

15e   Vocabulary in Textbooks

Textbooks often introduce many new terms related to the subject of the book. In fact, much of learning a subject is learning its special vocabulary. You cannot progress in mathematics, for example, without knowing the terms *calculate, congruent,* and *theorem;* in psychology without learning definitions for words like *perception, cognition,* and *motivation;* in literature without learning the meaning of words like *genre, metaphor,* and *irony.*

Thus in many disciplines, if you learn the new technical vocabulary, you have learned a large part of the subject. To introduce specialized vocabulary, textbooks use many strategies for presenting vocabulary and helping you learn it. Drawing on the vocabulary teaching techniques of textbooks can help you learn the subject more rapidly and can help you prepare for examinations by isolating important terms.

Special Vocabulary in Your Textbooks

Vocabulary Types	*Examples*
Technical terms to identify objects	anatomy text identifying body parts: *femur, patella*
Familiar objects broken down into less familiar parts	biology text labeling cell parts: *nucleus, membrane*

Processes important to the subject	government text explaining *judicial review, congressional oversight*
Concepts important to the subject	sociology text defining *role models, reference groups*

Term Identification and Definition

Often writers use **boldface** or *italics* the first time a new term of importance appears in a textbook. Then a definition frequently follows in that sentence—in parentheses or through other punctuation—or in a separate sentence. A discussion of how the term then applies to the subject matter and to related terms also may appear. In some books, definitions of new terms appear in the margin or as a footnote on the same page.

One way to classify matter is based on chemical composition. Some substances, called **pure substances**, have the same chemical composition throughout and from sample to sample, and they cannot be separated into their components by physical means (those not involving chemical reactions). A form of sand called silica, for example, is composed of silicon combined with oxygen in specific proportions. Different grains of silica sand vary in size but have the same composition.

—James P. Birk

Linked Definitions

At times several terms with related definitions appear together in the same paragraph. Understanding how the words are related to each other can help you understand each of the terms better. Note the use of boldface print to identify the new vocabulary.

Cost is the price that a business pays for a product. **Selling price** is the price for which a business sells a product to a customer. The difference between selling price and cost is called **markup.** Markup is added to a retailer's cost to cover the expenses of operating a business. Markup is usually expressed as a percent of the retailer's cost. This percent is called the **markup rate.**

The basic markup equations used by a business are

Selling price = cost + markup
$$S \quad = C + M$$

Markup = markup rate × cost
$$M \quad = \quad r \quad \times C$$

—Richard Aufmann and Vernon Barker

Vocabulary Diagrams

A common way to introduce and define new vocabulary, especially in the sciences and technology, is to provide a labeled diagram. The diagram identifies the various parts of an object, giving each a name. Not only do these identify exactly and concretely what each term means; they also provide a visual image that may help you remember each term and how it relates to the other terms labeled in the same diagram. This illustration of the digestive system on page 173 identifies vocabulary visually.

Glossaries and Word Lists

Often textbooks so depend on the vocabulary of a subject that a glossary—a list of new terms and definitions—will appear at the start or end of each chapter or at the end of the book. These lists help you review new terms as well as your knowledge of concepts, objects, and topics in the subject area. The glossary excerpt on the next pages comes from a psychology textbook.

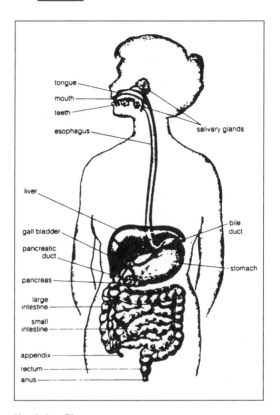

Vocabulary Diagram

Somatoform disorders Psychological disorders in which the major symptoms are physical complaints of illness, fatigue, discomfort, or paralysis.

Conversion disorders Disorders in which the sufferer reports a loss of movement or sensation in some part of the body, for which there is no neurological basis.

Somatization disorders Disorders in which the individual complains of vague physical symptoms—such as fatigue, dizziness, and headaches—that have no physical basis.

> **Dissociative disorders** A group of psychological disorders in which the individual is unable to remember recent events, his or her identity, or parts of his or her personality.
>
> —*James D. Laird and Nicholas S. Thompson*

Nouns in Academic Subjects

Since so much of an academic subject has to do with naming things, many important terms appear as *nouns*. (Nouns are "naming" words for persons, places, or things.) Simple actions, such as *cancel* (as in "cancel an order") become names of action—*cancellation* in this case. Descriptions of objects, such as *pure*, turn into names of general qualities, such as *purity*. Or, to stay with the word *pure*, we can use it to name actions related to a pure state, such as *purify*. Then we can change the converted word into a general process name, such as *purification*. If you read any of these complex noun forms, think of the term in its simplest root form. The process of turning words into noun forms is called *nominalization*.

Note the simple form of the word as the basis for the noun forms in psychology:

Word (Simple Form)	Noun Forms (Nominalized Word)
behave	behavior
	behavioral
	behaviorism
depress	depression
	depressive
	depressional
operate	operant
	operative
	operability
	operational

Word (Simple Form)	Noun Forms (Nominalized Word)
stress	stressful
	stressor
	stress-inducer
sense	sensory
	sensorimotor
	sensitivity
	sensate
	sentient
	sensitive
	sensation

In the following selection on theories of supposed biological causes of crime, you can determine meanings of italicized words by using the various vocabulary clues explained in this chapter. Definitions for the words appear in the margin. Which clues or combination of clues indicated the meanings shown—particular context clues (**2c**), word-part clues (**2d**), denotation and connotation (**2e**), or shades of meaning (**2f**)?

Criminals—Born or Bred?

The notion that, one way or another, "criminals are born" has a certain appeal, for it offers a simple answer to a complex problem. Not too surprisingly, many attempts have been made over the years to explain crime in terms of biological factors.

In the early twentieth century, it was widely assumed that criminals suffered from "moral insanity" or some other form of inherited *degeneracy*. In 1911, for example, the Italian *criminologist* Cesare Lombroso declared that criminals typically had such features as shifty

degeneracy fallen moral quality
criminologist a person who studies crime

receding moving backward
evolutionary development of life forms
instincts inborn patterns of behavior

periodically from time to time

disproportionately more than expected
presumably assumed to be
facilitated helped
distinctive noticeably different
genetic relating to biological inheritance
abnormalities features that are not usual
chromosome the chemical bearer of genetic information

eyes, *receding* hairlines, strong jaws, and red hair—apparently the results of an *"evolutionary* throwback" that produced "ferocious *instincts"* and "an irresistible craving for evil." Research soon showed, however, that these physical features did not appear any more frequently in criminals than in the general population.

Biological theories of crime have reappeared *periodically* since Lombroso's time. In the 1940s and 1950s William Sheldon and his associates reported that juvenile delinquents in Boston seemed *disproportionately* likely to have a muscular, agile build—which *presumably facilitated* their involvement in such activities as gang fights, burglaries, or muggings. This finding caused some interest—until further research showed that there was nothing particularly *distinctive* about the delinquents' typical body types. Then, in the 1960s, attention switched to *genetic abnormalities* that were found in a few violent criminals: unlike normal males, who have an X and a Y *chromosome,* these criminals had an extra Y chromosome, giving them the combination XYY. Researchers investigated this possible genetic factor, only to find that the apparent link was a coincidence: there is no consistent association between the extra chromosome and criminality.

SOURCES: Cesare Lombroso, *Crime: Its Causes and Remedies* (Boston: Little, Brown, 1911); William H. Sheldon et al., *Varieties of Delinquent Youth* (New York: Harper and Row, 1949); Sheldon Glueck and Eleanor Glueck, *Physique and Delinquency* (New York: Harper and Row, 1956); Ian Taylor et al., *The New Criminology* (London: Routledge and Kegan Paul, 1973).

—*Ian Robertson*

Subject Index

Main ideas
 compared with topics, 60–61
 directly stated, 61–64
 as generalizations, 108
 identifying, 4
 implied, 61, 64–70
 outlining, 137
 in note taking, 136
 in paragraphs, 59–70
 in sentences, 55–59, 61–64
 in summaries, 139–140, 141
 reading for, 55–70, 72
 underlining, 133
Maps, 49–51. *See also*
 Illustrations; Visual aids
Margin notes, 132–135
Matching questions, 149
Meanings
 context clues to, 161–163
 and generalization, 104–110
 shades of, 169–170
 word-part clues to, 164–167
Mood, 121
Multiple-choice questions,
 149–150

Negative terms, 123
Nominalization, 174–176
Note taking, 4, 135–136. *See also*
 Outlining
 underlining/highlighting and,
 132–135
Nouns, 174–176

Opinions
 author, 72
 compared with facts, 112–118
 conclusions from, 103
 evidence supporting, 118–119
 and journal writing, 142–145
 signal words for, 117
Order of importance, 80–81
Outcomes, predicting, 96–103.
 See also Generalization

Outlining, 137–138

Pace, 120
Paragraphs
 defined, 59
 main ideas in, 59–70
 organization of, 72
 patterns of, 78–88
 summarizing, 139–141
Photographs, 40–44. *See also*
 Illustrations; Visual aids
Place order, 79–80
Point of view, 121–122
Prefaces, 22, 25
Prefixes, 164, 165–166
Prejudiced writing, 122–124
Prereading, 2–4, 9–14
Previewing, 9, 17–21. *See also*
 Surveying
 parts of books, 22–27
Prior knowledge, 2, 9–10
Processes, vocabulary of, 171
Propaganda, 122–123
Punctuation, 162
Purpose, in writing, 121

Questions
 accompanying readings, 7
 essay, 146, 150–155
 for evaluating evidence, 119
 for fact-finding, 72–73
 fill-in, 149
 for finding main ideas in
  sentences, 56
 for idea evaluation, 111
 for making inferences, 94
 matching, 149
 multiple-choice, 149–150
 prereading and, 3–4
 in prereading, 13–14
 previewing, 18
 short-answer, 146, 147–150
 in SQ3R, 129
 textbook study, 16

Author Index

CREDITS

Page 19: Photo © David R. Frazier Photolibrary. **Page 24:** From *Contemporary Business Communications,* Second Edition, by Scot Ober. Copyright © 1995 by Houghton Mifflin Company. Used by permission. **Page 25:** Reprinted with permission from *Good Dirt: Confessions of a Conservationist* by David Morine. Copyright © 1990 by David E. Morine. Published by the Globe Pequot Press, Old Saybrook, CT. **Page 26:** From *Contemporary Business Communications,* Second Edition, by Scot Ober. Copyright © 1995 by Houghton Mifflin Company. Used by permission. **Page 28:** From *Building Bridges* by William B. Gudykunst et al. Copyright © 1995 by Houghton Mifflin Company. Used by permission. **Pages 29–30:** From *Making America* by Carol Berkin et al. Copyright © 1995 by Houghton Mifflin Company. Used by permission. **Pages 31–33:** From *The Challenge of Democracy,* Fourth Edition, by Kenneth Janda et al. Copyright © 1995 by Houghton Mifflin Company. Used by permission. **Pages 34–35:** From *Business,* Fourth Edition, by William M. Pride, Robert Hughes, and Jack R. Kapoor. Copyright © 1993 by Houghton Mifflin Company. Used by permission. **Page 37:** From *Collected Poems* by Frank O'Hara. Copyright © 1958 by Maureen Granville-Smith, Administratrix of the Estate of Frank O'Hara. Reprinted by permission of Alfred A. Knopf, Inc. **Pages 36–38:** From *One World of Literature,* edited by Shirley Geok-Lim and Norman Spencer. Copyright © 1993 by Houghton Mifflin Company. Used by permission. **Pages 41–44:** From *Psychology,* First Edition, by Douglas Bernstein et al. Copyright © 1988 by Houghton Mifflin Company. Used by permission. **Page 45:** From McLaren et al., *Spaceship Earth: Life Science,* revised edition. Copyright © 1981 by Houghton Mifflin Company. Reprinted by permission of McDougal Littell Inc. All rights reserved. **Pages 52–54:** "Practicing or Not, Many Identify with Religion" "USA Remains Solidly Religious" by Desda Moss. Copyright © 1991, *USA Today.* Reprinted with permission. **Page 67:** From *Marketing: Basic Concepts and Strategies,* Ninth Edition, by William Pride and O. C. Ferrell. Copyright © 1995 by Houghton Mifflin Company. Reprinted by permission. **Page 68:** From *Sources of the Western Tradition,* Third Edition, by Marvin Perry, Joseph R. Peden, and Theodore H. Von Laue. Copyright © 1995 by Houghton Mifflin Company. Reprinted by permission. **Page 70:** Excerpted from *Economics,* First Edition, by William Boyes and Michael Melvin, copyright © 1991 by Houghton Mifflin Company. Reprinted by permission. **Pages 73–75:** Seth Mydans, "20th Century Lawsuit Asserts Stone Age Identity" by Seth Mydans. Copyright © 1988 by *The New York Times Company.* Reprinted by permission. **Page 90:** Photo © Lauren Freudman/Woodfin Camp and Associates. **Page 98:** From Thomas V. DiBacco, Lorna C. Mason, and Christian G. Appy, *History of the United States.* Copyright © 1991 by Houghton Mifflin Company. Reprinted by permission of McDougal Littell Inc. All rights reserved. **Pages 114–116:** From *Marketing: Basic Concepts and Strategies,* Ninth Edition, by William Pride and O. C. Ferrell. Copyright © 1995 by Houghton Mifflin Company. Reprinted by permission. **Pages 134–135:** "Where Does Money Come From?" from *The Browser's Book of Beginnings* by Charles Panati. Copyright © 1984 by Charles Caroll Hudson. Reprinted by permission of the author. **Pages 143–145:** From *A History of Western Society,* Fifth Edition, by John McKay et al. Copyright © 1995 by Houghton Mifflin Company. Used by permission. **Page 173:** Vocabulary diagram from McLaren et al., *Spaceship Earth: Life Science,* revised edition. Copyright © 1981 by Houghton Mifflin Company. Reprinted by permission of McDougal Littell Inc. All rights reserved. **Pages 175–176:** From Ian Robertson, *Sociology,* Third Edition. Worth Publishers, New York, 1987. Reprinted with permission.